Henry Paul Prescott

Strong Drink and Tobacco Smoke

The Structure, Growth, and Uses of Malt, Hops, Yeast, and Tobacco

Henry Paul Prescott

Strong Drink and Tobacco Smoke
The Structure, Growth, and Uses of Malt, Hops, Yeast, and Tobacco

ISBN/EAN: 9783743384316

Manufactured in Europe, USA, Canada, Australia, Japa

Cover: Foto ©Andreas Hilbeck / pixelio.de

Manufactured and distributed by brebook publishing software (www.brebook.com)

Henry Paul Prescott

Strong Drink and Tobacco Smoke

STRONG DRINK

AND

TOBACCO SMOKE;

THE STRUCTURE, GROWTH, AND USES OF MALT, HOPS, YEAST, AND TOBACCO.

WITH ONE HUNDRED AND SIXTY-SEVEN ORIGINAL ILLUSTRATIONS, DRAWN AND ENGRAVED ON STEEL.

BY

HENRY P. PRESCOTT, F.L.S.

New York:
WILLIAM WOOD & CO.
1870.

PREFACE.

MUCH of the matter contained in the following pages formed the subject of a lecture, delivered on various occasions to country audiences, in which the attempt was made to popularise an interesting branch of science: Plant structure, life, and growth. For this purpose it mattered little what plants should be selected as illustrations, but it appeared to me, on reflection, that those which form the basis of our "Strong Drink and Tobacco Smoke" (the title chosen for the lecture) would prove more interesting and instructive than so-called less useful plants.

The introduction of the tobacco leaf as a subject for analysis was thought desirable, in these days of universal smoke, as affording an illustration of the simple means necessary to detect its spurious substitutes; thus enabling the smoker to become, if he choose, his own analyst. It affords an opportunity to display some striking illustrations of the variations which Nature elaborates in the minutiæ of the leaves of plants.

Practical men—farmers, brewers, and maltsters—will, I think, find in the pages of the book some hints which may prove of value, as suggestive of the waste of material constantly occurring in the granary, the brewery, and the malthouse.

Whilst divesting any subject of the technicalities of scientific language, I have endeavoured to be strictly accurate as to facts, and the definitions of them.

For the rest, Nature may speak for herself in her own eloquent language, through her works and the marvels of them.

HENRY PRESCOTT, F.L.S.

St. John's Wood.
July 1868.

EDITOR'S PREFACE.

THOUGH having no special knowledge of the subject treated of in this book, I have endeavoured to see it safe through the press for the sake of its writer, who was a very old friend of mine. The son of an actor who stood high in the estimation of the past generation of playgoers, but who died while his children were young, Henry Paul Prescott was very early thrown upon the world to shift for himself. Gifted with much natural taste and feeling for art, he tried as a boy to carve out a career for himself among the painters. But before starvation overtook him, he was fortunate enough to find shelter in the Excise. Mr. Wood, long the chairman of the Board, who had known his father and always took a kindly interest in the fortunes of Prescott and his elder brother, providing places for both in the service over which he presided.

It was while serving in the lower grades of the Inland Revenue hierarchy that my friend acquired the familiarity with the character of malt, hops, and tobacco, which is evidenced in the following paper.

He took to the microscope, partly for the love of it, partly for its usefulness in his profession, and partly, I think, because it gave him an excuse for the practice of etching, an art of which he was passionately fond, and in which the plates which accompany this work show that he had attained no mean proficiency.

For years past the preparation of these plates, and of the text which accompanies them, had been the solace and occupation of his leisure; and it was his great ambition to publish them. But a few months ago he fell into a rapid consumption, that which carried off his elder brother twenty years ago, and died without having seen more than the first sheet in type.

Critical readers will note much room for improvement in the text of the little book; but on the whole, it seemed to me better not to attempt to do more than remove obvious errors, or supply the place of obvious deficiencies in a work which pretends to be but an imperfect memorial of an incomplete life.

T. H. HUXLEY.

CONTENTS.

CHAPTER I.
INTRODUCTORY 1

CHAPTER II.
MATERIALS 9

CHAPTER III.
HOW BARLEY GROWS 17

CHAPTER IV.
STRUCTURE OF BARLEY AND SOME OTHER SEEDS . . . 32

CHAPTER V.
HOPS AND YEAST 39

CHAPTER VI.
MALT, BEER, SPIRIT 51

CHAPTER VII.
TOBACCO AND SOME OTHER LEAVES . . . 63

LIST OF PLATES.

Vertical section of Coffey's Distilling Apparatus . . . . . . *To face p.* 56

PLATE I.

Figs. 1. A representation in miniature of an inflated sheep bladder.—2. Part of same cut across its length.—3. A collection of same supposed to be held together.—4. A vegetable cell with two rings formed in its interior.—5. Another, with six rings.—6. Four cells super-imposed, united to form a tube.—7. Dotted ducts.—8. A vegetable vessel with deposit formed on its interior in a spiral curve.—9. Spiral vessels from leaf veins.—10. A reticulated vessel.—11. A scalariform duct. —12. A double-pointed wood cell.—13. A square-ended wood cell.— 14. A collection of same as *tissue.*—15. A pitted cell from a deal shaving.—16. A part of a single-pointed wood fibre.—17. A branched wood fibre.—18. A pointed ditto.—19. A branched fibre from woody portion of a seed-coat.—20. An oblong cell from skin of leaf.—21. Two irregularly-shaped cells from skin of leaf.—22. Two irregularly-shaped cells from the skin of *Cocculus Indicus.*—23. A cell with wavy outline, from skin of leaf, under side.—24. Kidney-shaped cells from skin of leaf forming a *stoma.*—25. Same viewed in vertical section.

PLATE II.

Figs. 1. A grain of barley with the husks removed from lower end to show *the Embryo.*—2 to 8. Grains of barley in different stages of development.—9. The young barley-plant.—10. A young rootlet.—11. A newly-formed leaf with *strap.*—12. Portion of a fully-developed leaf of barley.—13. A minute portion of a leaf blade cut transverse-vertically.—14. A horizontal section of barley stem.—15. A vertical section of the same.—16. A minute portion of skin of young straw with *hairs* developing.

PLATE III.

FIGS. 17. A barley plant.—18. Part of same divided down the centre, showing the size and position of *inflorescence*.—19. The same, showing the divisions of the *inflorescence* into undeveloped and developing portions.—20. *Inflorescence* in a very rudimentary condition.—21. Further development of same into lobed masses.—22. More advanced *inflorescence*.—23. One of the lobes developed into a perfect flower.—24. Ovary and one stamen separated.

PLATE IV.

FIGS. 25. A vertical section of mature barley straw.—26. A portion of *silicated* epidermis or skin from mature stem, showing the curved prickly hairs.—27. A portion of the epidermis of a leaf without hairs.—28. A minute portion of a very young awn, with spiral vessels and young hairs developing.—29. A diagram showing the position of the inflorescence relatively to the surrounding leaves.—30. Portion of barley ear showing the lateral supports by which each grain is protected.—31. *Pollen granules.*

PLATE V.

FIGS. 1. A grain of barley.—2. Another (damaged) grain.—3. Another (perfect) grain.—4. The *needle*.—5. Hard silicated hairs from its borders.—6. *The tuft* removed from base of grain.—7. The position of the tuft relatively to the embryo when the grain is cut across.—8. A minute portion of wing of tuft, showing the cellular tissue to which the long delicate filaments are attached.—9. Section of seed through the embryo.—10. Horizontal section of upper or leaf portion of embryo.—11. Ditto, of portion forming rootlets.—12. Starch granules from albumen of seed.

PLATE VI.

FIGS. 13. Seed coats of barley seeds.—14. Silica plates on outer layer of cells of skin when dry.—15. The same after the grain has been steeped in water for some time.—A *strobile* or fruit of the Hop.—17. A bract of same, showing the position of: 18. The seed at its base.—19. Seed with investing membrane to show the *lupulite*, very abundant on this membrane.—20, 21.—Seed divested of membrane viewed in face and on edge.—22. A granule of *lupulite* burst with dilute sulphuric acid.—23. A portion of a fruit of brewer's spent-hops, showing the position of the seeds and lupulite grains unaffected by boiling.—24. A minute portion of the seed pellicle or base of bract (17), beset with lupulite.

PLATE VII.

FIGS. 1. A grain of Cocculus Indicus.—2. A diagram of the seed constructed from dissections.—3. A grain of Paradise.—4. A diagram of the seed.—5. Oil globules from the large *cysts*.—6. A grain of Datura Stramonium.—7. A horizontal diagram of the seed.

PLATE VIII.

Figs. 25. A minute portion of a Hop leaf.—26. The seed of the Hop.—27, 28. Portions of the acorn-cup of the Valonia Oak.—29, 30. Branched and simple hairs.

PLATE IX.

Figs. 1. A leaf Virginian Tobacco attached to stem.—2. Portion of skin from under surface.—3. Hairs separated.—4. A transverse-vertical section of portion of leaf-blade, with hairs and breathing pores on under surface.—5. A horizontal section of midrib of leaf.—6. A leaf of Burdock.—7. Hairs from under surface of leaf terminating in long delicate filaments.—8. Horizontal section of midrib of leaf with lobed outline, and bundles of woody fibre separated.—9. Leaf of Dock, the stipule at base of stalk detached.—10. Club-shaped, striated hairs, from skin of midrib and veins.—11. Horizontal section of midrib, with lobed surface, and woody bundles separated.—12. A portion of skin of under side of leaf blade.

PLATE X.

Figs. 1. A leaf of Chicory.—2. A horizontal section from midrib of leaf, with thin woody bundles.—3. A portion of the skin removed from under side of leaf.—4. Leaf of Comfrey.—5. Horizontal section of midrib of leaf, showing the position and character of woody bundles.—6. A minute portion from the skin of the leaf on its under side.—7. Leaf of Jerusalem Artichoke.—8. Horizontal section of midrib of leaf, with woody bundles.—9. Epidermis from under side of leaf.

STRONG DRINK AND TOBACCO SMOKE.

CHAPTER I.

INTRODUCTORY.

"To eat, drink, and be merry," whilst life lasts, appear to be instincts of man's nature, scarcely requiring the sanction or the recommendation of a proverb; but from the hurried toil of life in which too many of us eat our daily bread, it may be good and refreshing to rest awhile, and turn to the green hill-side, to "look at the lilies of the field how they grow."

There we shall see all living objects, whether it be the insect on the wing in drowsy flight, or the bird up yonder carolling his song as if in praise and thanksgiving for the permission of life in this beautiful world; whether it be the humble plants of the varied thousands that adorn our English hedgerow:—

"A violet by a mossy stone
Half hidden from the eye;"

or the countless roses of delicate hue that adorn its summit—or, in the ditch beneath it, the brilliant flowers of the water-crowfoot, lying in graceful repose on its outspread leaves, whilst its silken tresses sway gently from side to side with the eddying current underneath; all these, as parts of animated Nature, fulfilling with thorough steadfastness of purpose the conditions for which they were called into being, a full and vigorous life, and so contributing their share to the enjoyments of man. Viewed thus, the most familiar objects of life that surround us afford ample scope for the attainment of real knowledge, exercise for thought, and an inexhaustible field for inquiry and research.

On the other side of that hedgerow lies a field of growing barley, and two fields beyond it, the graceful hop plants rear high in air their dazzling green festoons, stretching from pole to pole. Perhaps no two plants, since the world began, have had so great a moral influence on the human race; it may be that no other two products of nature, varied and beautiful as these are, ever so gladdened or made sad the hearts of men; for if to the fruit of these two plants we add another, the humble yeast plant, all the ingredients are present from which "strong drink," whisky, and beer, are obtained.

I purpose, therefore, to trace the life history of the barley plant, from its earliest growth to maturity and death, giving a description of the structure and minute anatomy of the root, stem, leaves, and seed. I shall show the careful provision which Nature has made for the healthy life of the plant in every stage of its growth, more particularly during its most critical period, the flowering, and maturing of the seed.

A careful examination of hop-fruit will show in what part of it is lodged the bitter principle, so valuable to the brewer, and, incidentally, it will be seen how much of it he unconsciously wastes. The nature and action of the yeast plant, with a glance at its use in the brewery and distillery, and a sketch of the "patent apparatus" by which English whisky is distilled at the rate of several thousand gallons per hour, will complete the chapters on strong drink.

Whilst smoking my pipe with you, reader, I will mix a leaf or two (literally "weeds") with your best cavendish, and when our cloud is blowing we will put our heads together, and try if we can find out what those "weeds" are.

Barley seed, when converted into malt, forms the practical ingredient of our strongest drinks—whisky, gin, and beer; and, although many other seeds of plants, such as rye, maize, oats, &c., can be malted, yet none are found so profitable for this purpose as barley.

And here, at the very outset of our inquiries, we may well be struck with astonishment : 1. At the fact that these seeds, which, when broken open, consist apparently of nothing but a fine white flour, surrounding a small conical body scarcely so large as a small pin's head, should, by being steeped in cold water for a few hours, become endowed with the marvellous power of strong healthy growth, even when free from contact with the earth. Though by no means difficult to observe in what part of the seeds this vital activity commences, or to demonstrate, with the assistance of the microscope, that the seeds of barley, like the plants which they produce, are nothing more than a collection of minute cells, we are nevertheless, after doing so, but a little nearer to the solution of those mighty mysteries which are included in the word, Life, although we have arrived at a comprehension of some of those agencies which produce its earliest manifestation.

This, though matter too deep for our philosophy, need not deter us from seeking the knowledge of other facts connected with the life of our barley plant, nor of studying some of the most beautiful provisions which Nature has made for the conservation and reproduction of a plant, that may be said to have become one of the staple necessities of society at the present time.

A special interest attaches, too, to the hop plant, as the source from which are derived the bitter and aromatic qualities for which English beers are prized, as the finest in the world. The dried fruit of this plant yielded, until recently, an enormous revenue to Government. It is, however, peculiarly liable to the attacks of the "fly," or "blight," and, on this account, it became so difficult to collect the hop duty, that it has been abandoned by the Government.

Yeast, with which both our bread and our beers are fermented, takes its place in the vegetable kingdom as a plant very low in its organization, but nevertheless immensely rapid in its growth, and appearing to require exactly the medium which is supplied by a saccharine solution, such as that of malt or mixed grain, for its continuous development.

From these three plants, then, we get our "strong drink," and it is a remarkable circumstance, that to use them in the manufacture of our beer, as in brewing, or of our whisky, the distilled spirit, we have to begin where Nature does—to grow the barley and yeast plants. In generating barley to convert it into malt, or in adding yeast to the brewer's worts to excite fermentation, we but imitate the earliest processes of actual plant-growth, though in both cases the operations are, at a certain stage, suddenly arrested. The result of fermentation, as is well known, is the production of the intoxicating element of both beer and whisky—alcohol—which is left mixed with saccharine matter, and hopped by the brewer; or separated from it in its more concentrated and purer state by the distiller.

Such, then, are the bases of our strong drink. I fear that our tobacco will not always bear so satisfactory an analysis. The reason of this is obvious. The temptation to adulterate tobacco is very strong, and will ever remain so whilst the tax on importation bears such an enormous ratio to the value of the taxed material, as that of a 3s. tax on tobacco leaves worth from 6d. to 1s. per pound. Besides, not one person in one hundred, or, it may safely be stated, in one thousand, has the slightest acquaintance with the general features and characters of genuine tobacco. Most of us, therefore, must be powerless in the hands of the fraudulent manufacturer, to whom we not unfrequently pay something more than 3s. 6d. per pound for the leaves of wayside plants—dock, burdock, foxglove, elecampane, &c. &c.—with which our tobacco leaves are, at times, contaminated. If it is somewhat unpleasant to be thus reminded of what we may be smoking, it is equally satisfactory to know that very little patience and attention are all that are requisite to gain a knowledge of those marked and unchangeable characters which Nature has stamped on the leaves of plants, as on all her productions; and thus, those of them invisible to the naked sight can, with the help of a microscope, be traced in our cigars, our cut tobaccos, and even in our snuffs. Nor is much learning requisite to master the few and simple features which characterize these leaves; for they are of so marked and constant a character, so easily to be understood, and the analysis of them lies so completely within the reach of ordinary intelligence, as to be well worth the trouble of acquiring.

And this leads me to the manner of treating my four plants. A cursory glance at some of the numerous illustrations of the book, will impress many readers with a notion that the objects delineated are as strange-looking as they are novel; but they are not, on that account, difficult to understand, or, as I believe, unworthy of being studied. Prominent among these will be found sections, or slices, of the various parts of the plants under consideration, and in every instance they are intended to represent their structure in a given direction. For instance, in order to trace the growth of the barley plant, we must begin by placing the seeds in moist earth, or in water, for a day or two, and then watch their germination, and the gradual development from day to day of the young plants. The examination of the tissues composing the leaves and the straw, in their gradual development, will exhibit some most interesting structures under the microscope. Carrying our researches a step farther, the germs of the future flowers of the plant may be easily discovered, and these traced to their fructification and ultimate development into mature seeds; thus completing the cycle of the plant's life from a seed to the seed again. So, again, with the hop plant; if the leaves and bracts of the fruit are examined with a magnifying glass, our admiration is immediately aroused by the beautiful form, colour, and arrangement upon their surfaces, of thousands of minute golden-coloured, granular bodies, which contain the *lupulite*, so valuable to the brewer.

Descending to the lowest region of vegetable life, we have the yeast plant, whose marvellous development from simple *cells* into long threads or filaments, by cell-division and multiplication, may actually be watched on the field of the microscope, when the plant is fed with a solution of sugar.

The external characters of tobacco leaves contrast

curiously with those of other plants. Interesting on this account, they become even more so when examined under the microscope. We then see the never-ending variations which Nature elaborates in the internal structure of the leaves of plants, no less than in the form and characters of the minute, invisible hairs with which their surfaces are adorned; these last serving us, even when the leaves have been pounded to dust, as infallible records of the plant which has produced them.

In short, search where we will in Nature's laboratory, her surprising variations of form, her myriad methods of varying minutiæ, excite our wonder at every step we take in the endeavour to unravel these hidden beauties.

CHAPTER II.

MATERIALS.

BEFORE proceeding to grow our barley seeds in order to obtain young plants for the examination of their tissues, it will be necessary to give a brief sketch of the elements of which plants generally are composed.

Let Plate 1, fig. 1, represent, on a very large scale, a minute bladder, distinguishable only as such by the aid of a microscope. This, when cut across at a right angle to the direction of its length, or horizontally, would have the appearance represented at fig. 2, seen in perspective. Suppose a number of such bladders to be held together at certain points of their surfaces, and their ends to lie in different planes; if a knife-blade were passed through them, as in the previous instance, the section would have the appearance represented at fig. 3. A second cut through such a tissue, in the direction of the transverse line, would divide three of the bladders just above their ends, and would escape the other two. Now we have only to call these suppositious bladders vegetable *cells*, and their skins the *cell-walls* (in nature much more transparent than these skins), and we have a tolerable illustration of the composition of the soft, juicy parts of most plants, that is to say, *cellular tissues*, and the illustration will further show the vacant or intercellular spaces, where the cell-walls do not infringe upon each other. When such a section as that included between the upper surface and the line *a*, fig. 3, is placed under the microscope (supposing it to be sufficiently thin and transparent to transmit light), it is evident that the side walls of five of the cells will be visible, and the ends only of two.

But many plant cells possess the singular property of forming on the inner surface of their walls a deposit, which takes sometimes very eccentric and very beautiful forms. Of these the most simple is that of a ring or rings, as in the cells found in many of the *Cacti*, one of which is represented at fig. 4, in which two such rings occur, serving probably to give it strength. Fig. 5 is another cell, with as many as six distinct rings visible on the inner surface of its wall. This deposit very frequently overlies almost the entire surface of the cell, leaving, where it is absent, minute dots which admit the light readily through them. Fig. 6 represents a row of such cells, which are also very abundant in elder pith, but possess fewer markings or dots.

Any or all these forms of cells, when collected together, as shown at fig. 3, form what is called, technically, a *cellular* tissue, as distinguishing it from another tissue common among plants and abundant in wood, which I will now describe.

In the growing parts of plants are found, in all stages of development, long tubes or *vessels*. These, in many instances, are seen to be formed by a series of cells placed one above another (Plate 1, fig. 6), their ends becoming finally obliterated, when they form canals or vessels, such as are represented at fig. 7, having their walls dotted. This description of vessel is called a *dotted duct*, and is very common in the roots of many plants, such as chicory.

Vessels, like cells, have their walls lined internally with a deposit. Fig. 8 represents one of them with such a deposit, in the form of a fibre wound spirally on its wall, the fibre having become stretched by the elongation of the vessel.

Beautiful examples of spiral vessels occur in the veins of leaves (fig. 9); they are abundant in the stem of the strawberry plant, and are readily seen by passing a knife-blade gently round the stem, and then dividing it by gradually drawing the parts asunder. The fine threads thus obtained, when examined under the microscope, will be found to consist of spiral vessels, with the fibres more or less unrolled at their extremities.

Another very common form of vessel (fig. 10) is known as *reticulated*, owing to the broken irregular form which the deposit assumes.

Fig. 11 represents portions of three vessels taken from the stem of the vine. These are called *scalariform* ducts, owing to the deposit being formed in bars, similar in appearance to the rungs of a ladder.

Groups of any or of all these forms of vessels (Plate 1, figs. 7—11) are known as *vascular tissue*, as distinguished from the *cellular* tissue above described.

The continuous growth of a plant is generally accompanied by the formation of wood; that is to say, much of the cellular tissue is supplanted by tougher and more unbending material, more suitable for the support of the plant during growth. These woody parts are mostly composed of long *fibrous* cells with thick walls. Fig. 12 represents one of them pointed at both ends, and fig. 13 another with nearly square ends. They occur in abundance in herbaceous plants, and in all wood knit together into a tissue, such as is seen at fig. 14. When united in one tissue with the vessels before described, the compound tissue is called *fibro-vascular*.

A common deal shaving exhibits, under the microscope, a tissue composed of long cells pointed at both ends, and having on their sides pits, or cup-shaped depressions (fig. 15), which in two individual cells are fitted face to face, and thus form a cavity for the reception of the resinous matter which we smell so perceptibly in freshly-cut deal, or in newly-planed deal shavings and sawdust.

A curious form of the fibrous cell is, according to some authors, found in bark (figs. 16, 17), some being branched. Fig. 18 is another form of fibrous cell, also found in bark, and like some cells *dotted*. In inner coats of seeds are commonly found minute, elongated cells that have coalesced to form long delicate fibres (Plate 1, fig. 19). Stringy, tough vegetables, with which we sometimes make unpleasant acquaintance, owe their unpalatableness to the large quantity of fibrous tissue which they contain.

The outer coverings or skins of herbaceous plants are very frequently composed of thick-sided, flat, tabular cells (figs. 20, 21). The upper surfaces of leaves are frequently covered with a thin pellicle of cellular tissue (fig. 22); their lower surfaces with a tissue composed of flat, tabular cells with wavy outlines (fig. 23).

Many readers will be surprised to learn that plants breathe principally through their leaves, but the experiments of philosophers have placed the fact beyond question. The delicate organisms by which this function is performed may be well seen by detaching a minute piece of skin from the under side of a leaf, and placing it in water under the microscope. These will be seen lying in great profusion amongst the peculiar flat tabular cells, with undulating outlines (fig. 23), peculiar to this part, as minute, kidney-shaped cells, touching at their ends and having a slit or minute opening between them. One of these, viewed from above, and greatly magnified, is seen at fig. 24, and cut through vertically at one point of their junction at fig. 25. As moisture is supplied to or withdrawn from the leaves either by imbibition or evaporation, these breathing pores (*stomates* as they are called) expand or contract, and in so doing partially close or open the slit, and so regulate the passage of moisture and gaseous matter from or to the interior of the leaf. Though very minute, they must, from the fact of thousands of them occurring within a square inch of surface, play a most important part physiologically in the life of the plant.

It is also on the skin of the leaf that the peculiar cellular appendages, *hairs*, are placed. These are found sometimes in two or three different forms on the same leaf, and although frequently invisible to the naked eye, are, from their excessive transparency, very beautiful objects under the microscope. Their forms and characters are as constant for each leaf as they are diversified in the leaves of different plants; and, as our investigations proceed, it will be seen how objects so simple as a hair may be made available in the analysis of tobacco leaves.

The plants and leaves, the structure of which we have now to study, are nothing more than variously disposed groups of cells and vessels held firmly together; I have now to describe briefly the manner in which they may be most profitably studied.

An architect, desirous of conveying an idea of the form and construction of the house he intends building, prepares very carefully a series of drawings, exhibiting ground plans and sections of the various parts of the proposed building. We, on the other hand, have to take to pieces the fabric which Nature has constructed, in order to obtain our ground plans and sections. This is accomplished by making careful sections of the plant from every part of it and in every direction of its growth, and submitting these to the searching power of the compound microscope, in order to view the structure from every point. For instance, a thin slice of the young green stem of barley cut horizontally (at a right angle to the direction of its growth), and placed in water on the stage of the microscope, will show whether the woody (*fibro-vascular*) tissues lie together in one mass, or are scattered in small wedge-shaped bundles (Plate 2, fig. 14). A thin slice from the same stem, cut vertically in the direction of its growth (Plate 2, fig. 15), will show the composition of its tissues, and from this, individual cells and vessels can be carefully dissected out under the dissecting microscope with two fine needles, for examination under the compound microscope, when their beautiful transparency will render their minutest structure very evident. If, in cutting these sections, the knife blade should by accident pass through (as it will do frequently) some part of a minute vessel in a somewhat slanting direction, the student will be rewarded with a view of a part of the interior of it, and will thus be enabled to compare the appearances of both surfaces. In fact, in this as in other matters, chance or accident will sometimes accomplish for us that which our most patient labour will not.

I shall have to speak of the method of examining leaf structure when treating of hops and tobacco, taking it for granted that the reader knows what books to read amongst the numerous published works on the microscope and its management. For the rest, successful study should depend less on books than on hearty desire and a strong will.

CHAPTER III.

HOW BARLEY GROWS.

Having given a general outline of the composition of a plant, the reader will be prepared to understand the process of growth of a simple grain of barley. If a grain be taken, and the outer husk and inner skin are removed from the thick end of it, on its smoother or ungrooved surface a small conical body will be found lodged in the white mealy portion of the grain, and darker than it. This is the *embryo* of a young plant (Plate 2, fig. 1) awaiting some exciting cause to bring its latent powers into action. Place a few of these grains whole in moist earth for three or four days, and watch the result. On examining the grain at the end of that time, it will be found that, although in external appearance it only exhibits a swollen appearance, yet, on opening it, or tearing away the husk, its internal characters have very much changed. Instead of the white mealy mass, we have a pasty-looking substance, the embryo has elongated considerably (fig. 2), and a number of slender filaments are protruding from the end of the grain, having burst through its husk. In two or three days more, if we remove the husk from another grain, we find a tough, almost horny structure, to which the little remaining mealy part of the grain most tenaciously adheres (fig. 3). This body is called the *cotyledon* or embryonic leaf. Growing as it were from this, and attached to it, is a small greenish conical body, another young leaf, whilst the extension in growth of the horny mass downwards forms the basis from which the young rootlets grow into the earth (Plate 2, figs. 4, 5). In a day or two, a still further development of the plant is seen; by removing the upper leaf, another still younger is found to have grown from the stem within it (fig. 6).

It will be observed, that one important feature of the plant's structure is illustrated in the growth of the leaves one *within* another, each younger one forcing the older one next to it in an outward direction. Fig. 7 represents a young plant about nine days old, removed bodily from the soil. The husk of the grain is still adhering slightly to the plant, but when this is removed (fig. 8), the contents of the grain are found to have undergone an entire change; instead of the white mealy mass which it once contained, its place is occupied by the bases of the leaves, and the tough horny substance to which these and the rootlets are fixed. The fact is, that the embryo, whilst growing, and forming rootlets and leaves, has evidently done so at the expense of the mealy portion of the grain—a beautiful provision that

Nature has made for the young plant, until it is able to assimilate other food.

The diagram (Plate 2, fig. 9) represents, on a much enlarged scale, a section of the young plant at the foregoing stage of its growth, cut open vertically, the leaves being represented by lines. There are six of these, exclusive of the cotyledonary leaf (c), and the figures 1 to 6 represent the order of their growth. No. 1, the first formed leaf, has been superseded in growth by No. 2, and has then died down; No. 2 in its turn will be outgrown by No. 3, and will then die down; and so with the others, the point from which they grow being a dense mass of living vegetable tissue. I shall have to return to this part of the subject when treating of the stem; in the meantime let us examine the rootlets of the plant. These are so delicate, that they may be placed bodily on the stage of the microscope in water, and pressed down under a thin glass cover. They will be found to consist of a mass of minute elongated cells, with very thin walls; in the centre of the mass spiral and other vessels are forming. But at the point of each rootlet is a peculiar conical body (fig. 10) called the *root cap*, which is supposed to assist materially in absorbing the salts and other matters held in the soil for the nourishment of the plant. This function is denied to it by many, but it is clearly proved that if these caps are broken off they are never reproduced and the rootlets wither.*

* Schleiden's Principles of Botany, p. 220.

The structure of the mature leaf will have to be considered presently. I draw attention now to the leaf in its youngest state, in order to illustrate a peculiarity in its structure that has a most important relation to the mechanical support of the entire plant. Examine one of the leaves of barley in as early a stage of its growth as possible (Plate 2, fig. 11), and here will be found, at the base of it, an elevated ridge of cellular tissue. This never lengthens to any great extent during the growth of the leaf, but it thickens considerably, and becomes, in a mature leaf, very tough and elastic. It is called the *strap* (figs. 11, 12 *st*), and performs the most useful office of preserving all that portion of the leaf which grows after it, for a time, in a cylindrical form. It thus encloses and protects the inner younger leaves (and, as we shall presently see, the flowers and fruit) until these, becoming too bulky, snap the strap asunder. The economy of Nature, vast as it is, can scarcely show a single contrivance more simple, or more admirably adapted for the purpose which it serves.

Fig. 13 represents a portion of a transverse-vertical section of a mature leaf of barley. In the centre of the section is the bundle of woody tissue (fibrous cells, spiral and other vessels) forming the middle vein of the leaf, and on either side of it three other such bundles running parallel to it. They are surrounded by loose cellular tissue, and enclosed or covered on both surfaces by abular-shaped cells, forming the upper and under skins of the leaf.

Plate 3, fig. 17, represents a young barley plant about six inches high. A slight swelling will be observed at one part of it, g. When cut open vertically its whole length (fig. 18), the stem is found to be perfectly hollow, excepting at certain points of it, where (as at a, b) diaphragms, or solid plates of cellular tissue, extend across it. Just above the upper one of these plates is a small, conical semi-transparent body, g. Fig. 19 is a highly-magnified representation of this part, which in reality is, at this time, no bigger than the head of a pin. Observe that all but the two inner leaves of the stem have been removed to show it more clearly. This minute body consists of two parts, and from it grow, by constant addition of new tissues, the inflorescence or flower axis, a (fig. 19), and b, the leaf axis or stem, the entire mass forming the terminal bud of the plant of which a and b are the flower and stem portions in a rudimentary state.

The mode of growth may be thus explained. Whilst the base of the terminal bud rested as it were on the diaphragm d, a leaf-bud was formed, and, on expanding into a leaf, the tissues from which it grew on the stem also increased and lengthened by the constantly renewed vitality imparted to them by the respiration of the leaf. By the time the stem has grown the length of the internode (fig. 18, a to b), the terminal bud has also increased in diameter, another leaf-bud is forming, and the plant repeats the process of horizontal and vertical growth.

At each point, where a new leaf-bud, and consequently

a new leaf, was produced, a solid plate of tissue (diaphragm) remains for a time; but as the diameter of each node of the stem increases, the central portion not being renewed, the stem in time becomes hollow.

In the centre of the lobed inflorescence (fig. 19, *a*) may be clearly distinguished, even at this early stage of its development, the flower and fruit-bearing stalk; at the base of this again is the last undeveloped joint of the stem, and beneath this the solid mass from which other leaves and internodes of the stem will be formed.

Plate 2, figs. 14 and 15, represent a horizontal and a vertical section of the mature green stem of barley. The sections are not cut across or through the middle of the last formed diaphragm, for then we should have a solid mass without the intervening space represented by the white ring which here separates the outer developing stem from the inner more immature portion, but at a point just above *d* (Plate 3, fig. 19).

The structure of the stem is well seen in the vertical section at Plate 4, fig. 25, where the spiral vessels are seen lying amongst the woody and dotted fibres, whilst the inner circular cells of the pith are gradually being torn asunder by the horizontal expansion of the stem at the internode above. The development of hairs on the outer skin may be easily traced on the young green stem. In early growth they have the appearance of minute knobs (Plate 2, fig. 16). When they are mature, and have become silicated on their outer surfaces, they have a more formidable appearance (Plate 4, fig. 26). They are most numerous on the green awns of the seed, where they may be seen in all stages of development (Plate 4, fig. 28 *h*).

A remarkable feature in the growth of our plants is the power they possess of absorbing from the soil, and secreting in their tissues, a very large amount of silica, the basis of flint-stones and of glass. In the ashes of barley straw De Saussure, a French chemist, found 57 per cent. of this substance; more recently our own illustrious chemist, Fownes, has given the analysis of straw from barley grown in Battersea Fields. When burned, it yielded 6·97 per cent. of unconsumed ashes. These ashes, on analysis, yielded in the soluble portion of them:—

Sulphate of potash	16·6	per cent.
Chloride and little silica	0·4	,,

In the insoluble portion:—

Siliceous scales	70·5	,,
Phosphates of lime and magnesia	8·5	,,
Carbonate of lime	2·0	,,
Alkali, magnesia, and loss	1·5	,,
Water	·5	,,
	100·0	

Of this silica, 87 per cent. was uncombined with any earthy or alkaline base.

Under the blow-pipe this silica may be made to fuse into a glass of topaz-yellow colour. Under the microscope it is seen as an extremely delicate transparent layer overlying and penetrating the cells of the outer skin, and is in many places rent and torn by the distension of this tissue (Plate 4, figs. 26, 27). Silica is one of those substances which the chemist finds some difficulty in obtaining in a perfectly pure state, yet we see our humble barley plant, in some most mysterious way, assimilating it in truly wonderful proportion.

I come now to the most interesting part of my subject. There are few people who do not take some interest in flowers. Those who do will not have failed, during a summer walk through a field of standing corn, to have seen and to have admired the wild poppy growing up amongst the forest of straw, and if they have plucked them, will recall to their minds those exquisite lines of Robert Burns, from his poem of "Tam O'Shanter:"—

> "But pleasures are like poppies spread,
> You seize the flower, the bloom is fled;
> Or, like snow-flakes on a river,
> A moment white, then lost for ever!"

All can appreciate the aptness of Burns' simile of fleeting pleasure, and the evanescent beauty of one of our loveliest wild plants; too often, the farmer would say, the close companion of growing barley. But from the eyes of Burns, as from our own, lay hidden many beautiful objects teeming with wealth for us. Though showing no outward signs of attractiveness, there yet lie carefully enfolded within the leaves of those green modest-looking barley plants, the germs of future flowers, and of fruit yet to be garnered. Plucking up a plant, root and all, and examining its exterior very carefully, a slight distension or swelling will be observed about midway ($g\ g$ Plate 3, fig. 17) up the stem. If the plant is now cut vertically through its entire length (fig. 18) a small conical, semi-transparent body, in reality no bigger than a pin's head (to which allusion was just now made in speaking of the stem), will be found at g. Fig. 19 c is a highly magnified representation of this body, which is the inflorescence, or flower-bearing portion of the plant, whilst still very young. When detached and more highly magnified it has the appeararance represented at fig. 20; that of a gelatinous, semi-transparent, conical body, with lobed margins. If we watch closely from day to day the development of this inflorescence, it will be found to increase rapidly in bulk, and to alter considerably in form.

Another stage of its growth is exhibited at fig. 21, in which the lobes are more strongly marked, and more numerous, and the mass has become broader. In a short time a still further development is observed (fig. 22), each lobe assuming distinct parts, the rudiments of floral leaves. Each lobe at length develops into a perfect flower (fig. 23), which, with its appendages, is something larger than the head of an ordinary pin, and of a pale yellow colour, with all its parts semi-transparent.

Whilst in this condition, the inflorescence is most

cautiously protected from violent accident or atmospheric influences. Plate 4, fig. 29, is a representation of a horizontal section of the plant through the inflorescence, and the surrounding leaves. In the drawing, the centre or midrib of each leaf, from the oldest to the youngest, is represented by the letters a, b, c, and if the convolutions of each leaf are traced, the leaves will be found to be so situated relatively to each other as to form five distinct coverings within which the inflorescence in the centre is. Truly this part of the plant's economy has been wonderfully contrived!

When mature, it will be seen that each lobe of the inflorescence has developed into a minute body, composed of three distinct parts, or *florets* (Plate 3, fig. 23). The two lateral ones (a a) are barren, and produce no seed; the central one is fertile, and consists of two outer scales (b b) with awns, which soon wither away; two other inner ones (d), enclosing a small body, the pistil, to which are attached, at its base, three oblong, yellowish bodies, with slender stalks; these are the stamens of the flower. We have here, then, a perfect flower with its reproductive organs, three stamens and a pistil. On opening one of the anthers of the stamens, a (fig. 24), there will be found lining its sides a quantity of fine yellow powder. This is known as pollen (Plate 4, fig. 31), and is the fertilizing principle of the flower.

At a certain period of the plant's growth, and whilst the inflorescence is yet protected by the sheathing leaves, these pollen granules fall from the anthers on to the feathery stigma (*st*) at the top of the ovary (Plate 3, *o*, fig. 24); they then thrust out long slender tubes, which penetrate the ovary through the style (*st*), and there discharge a viscid secretion which they contain. When thus impregnated, the embryo of a new plant is formed within the ovary, which becomes in time the seed. After impregnation, the stamens wither and fall off; the inner and outer scales of the flower close around the ovary, and become the inner and outer coats of the future barley-seed; and the barren florets (*a a*, 23) form, in time, the lateral appendages which help to keep the grains firmly fixed on their fruit-bearing stem (Plate 4, *a a*, 30).

Each lobe of the inflorescence having developed into a flower, the process explained takes place simultaneously, or nearly so, in each of them; and, in a short time afterwards, we see the green ear of barley bursting the strap of the uppermost and youngest leaf, which has, until now, enfolded it. It then bends downwards by its own weight, and is seen as the graceful ear of barley.

I found the fertilized ovaries to weigh, on an average, one-twentieth part of a grain, and the ripe, mature seed, seven-tenths of a grain; so that, from the time of the impregnation of the ovary to its maturity as seed, each ovary has increased its original weight thirteen times.

What particular office do the awns of the seed (fig. 30) fulfil in the economy of the plant? Comparing an ear of wheat with one of barley, the seeds of the former are found to be surrounded by several loosely-fitting coats (husks), which readily fall away on threshing, leaving the seeds naked. These serve as a sufficient protection from rain and atmospheric influences. In place of these, barley-seed, as we have seen, is furnished with two tightly-fitting tunics; and lest these should become damaged by moisture, they are furnished at their points with long, tapering awns, covered with minute hairs. The awns serve as admirable contrivances to carry off an excess of moisture, which might otherwise act injuriously on the seed. Such appears to me an explanation of the use of these very elegant appendages of the seed.

The use of the hairs, which are so abundant in the awns (and which, on reference to Plate 4, fig. 26, will be seen to curve outwards and upwards), is not so readily explained. The story is told of a youth who, whilst passing through a field of growing barley, carelessly snatched and placed in his mouth a few of these "barbed" awns. It so happened that they passed down the wind-pipe with the points of the hairs uppermost, which effectually prevented their dislodgment by coughing. This seemingly trifling incident led to violent hæmorrhage of the lungs, caused by these silicated hairs, and speedy death.

I have considered our barley plant hitherto as in a flourishing and healthy state of growth; but it, like other things, is subject to disease and death before reaching maturity.

Contrast, for instance, the two plants on the next page;

the one blooming with health, the ear just ready to leave its last loving support and covering, to bend downwards with its weight of fruit; the other, stark and stricken with a black disease, a lifeless and almost shapeless mass of cankering dust. This appearance is caused by *smut*, a fungus that attacks the barley plant during its flowering, and destroys what, but for it, had become a thing of beauty and of use.

The smut is a very fine black powder, which has entirely replaced the tissues that were developing into flower and seed; no trace of them being left, excepting such as hold together quite feebly a rude, shapeless mass, that was once almost a perfect flower. In what peculiar way this fungus settles on its victim it is difficult to imagine, for we have seen that the inflorescence of the plant is so carefully protected by the sheathing-leaves as to render any attack upon it from without, even by the deposit of minute germs floating in the air, scarcely possible. But there it is, all too plainly, and the reader may judge of its impalpable fineness when told that the figures represent the spores of this fungus in a dry state, and in water, magnified 400 diameters.

If I have been successful in describing the barley plant, and have made its life-history intelligible, the reader cannot fail to perceive how admirably Nature has adapted it for the growth and protection of its flowers. She has lodged them with amazing skill within a series of folding leaves, whose convolutions form around it a covering five times repeated. She has further endowed the plant with the wonderful power of abstracting silica from the soil in which it grows to harden and protect both stem and leaves with a nature as glistening as steel itself, and has so adapted its form and mode of growth as to suggest the utmost economizing of space : finally, to complete her fair work, ere its life is ended by the reaper's sickle, and its gracious fruit is gathered for our use, she has clothed it in golden hues to gild—

> "A gaily-chequered, heart-expanding view,
> Far as the circling eye can shoot around
> Unbounded, tossing in a field of corn."

CHAPTER IV.

STRUCTURE OF BARLEY AND SOME OTHER SEEDS.

ALMOST at the commencement of our studies, reader, we had occasion, whilst watching the development of the barley plant, to take particular notice of a minute body, the *embryo*, where we found vital activity first manifesting itself, after steeping the grain in cold water for a few hours.

A section of malt at that part of the grain in which this embryo is lodged is given at Plate 5, fig. 9. At s are the cells composing the two seed-coats of the grain; at a the white mealy portion (albumen), the cells of which have been freed from starch granules in nourishing the embryo; e is the embryo. This now consists of three folded leaves, in a rudimentary state, attached to a mass of vegetable matter, in which lie the undeveloped stem and rootlets. Horizontal sections of the embryo (figs. 10, 11), taken from above and below the centre of the embryo, exhibit these parts of its structure very plainly.

Looking at the outside of the base of the grain, on its grooved surface there will be observed a minute, very hard, conical body (Plate 5, *n*, fig. 1), to which, as I have never yet seen any description of it, I have given the name of the *needle*. If the base of the grain, that is, the part by which it was attached to the stalk when in the ear, remains undamaged in threshing, as in fig. 1, and the outer husk of it is removed after being soaked in water for a short time, there will be found lying on the inner coat a peculiarly formed, minute body, which I call the *tuft* (fig. 3, *t*). Separated from the grain, as at fig. 6, it is seen to consist of a central body of a spongy nature, furnished with two long arms, which, when considerably magnified, are resolved into plates of cellular tissue, furnished with innumerable long silky hairs.

Fig. 8 represents a portion of the extremity of one of the arms of the tuft.

From careful observation of many grains of barley, I have found that those which are damaged at their bases (fig. 2), in other words, whose ends are broken, seldom or ever contain the *tuft;* whilst those grains which have been more carefully threshed, and whose ends are perfect, invariably do. In examining such grains, after being steeped in water and allowed to dry, either naturally, or by artificial means, I have invariably found the tuft to contain amongst its filaments more or less of moisture, whilst all the rest of the seed is dry. We have then, I believe, in this minute body one of the essential elements for the successful cultivation or growth of the seed; it is, in fact, a true *sucker* to the seed, and when its position relatively to the embryo is considered, there can be little doubt that it fulfils the office of drawing water to the seed; and by the capillary attraction which its numerous delicate filaments offer to that medium, conveys it upwards to bathe the parts immediately surrounding the embryo.

It is well known that barley-seed communicates a strong tinge of its own colour to water in which it is steeped. The *tuft* lies immediately on the inner coat of the seed, and this coat consists of four layers of cells charged with coloured matter. By dissolving this, some peculiar action takes place on the starch of the albumen, by which the first phenomena of life are elicited and maintained. Barley - growers, brewers, maltsters, and distillers, having a special interest in the careful threshing of the grain, would do well, before purchasing samples for use, to examine the percentage of damaged corns it contains by means of a simple lens and a pair of needles.

The uses of the "needle" are not so apparent. It is very hard, highly silicated, and clothed with shorter and less elastic hairs than those on the tuft (Plate 5, fig. 4).

The seed-coats of barley offer some curious points for observation (Plate 6, fig. 13). The outer layers of elongated or fibrous tissue are covered externally with plates of silica, between which minute holes make their appearance, these being probably the points to which the bases of hairs were once attached To these cells succeed four or five rows of broad, tabular cells, which form the

outer coat. The inner one is made up of four or
five rows of long cells with very thin walls, forming
a thin pellicle, which lies on four rows of cells containing much colouring matter. These skins enclose
the large, irregularly-shaped cells, forming the albumen
in which an abundance of starch is lodged (Plate 5,
fig. 12). The silica plates on the outer layer of cells
separate at their edges, when the grain swells from
moisture (Plate 6, figs. 14, 15).

Cocculus Indicus (Plate 7, figs. 1 and 2).—In most
illegal companionship with our malt liquors are
frequently found the ground berries of the *Cocculus
Indicus*, which possess great stupifying and poisoning
power. The plant from which they are produced is a
native of Malabar and Eastern Islands of India, and
its fruit is imported to us in bags from Bombay, Madras,
and Ceylon.

Fig. 1 is a berry of the natural size, of a dark brown
colour, and corrugated surface. When examined under
the microscope, after careful dissection, its structure may
be thus described. The exterior skin is composed of three
or four layers of irregularly-shaped cells, with very thick
and dark-coloured walls (Fig. 2, *a*), overlying the woody
fibres (*b*) which are interlaced in every direction with
branching ligneous cells and spiral vessels (*sv*). Underlying these are the double-pointed, channeled, wood
cells, lying horizontally, with others interwoven per-
pendicularly to them (*d, g, e*) ; and underlying these is
a delicate pellicle formed of rows of delicate thin-walled

cells (*h*), which enclose the albumen (*c*), here seen full of minute starch grains; at (*f*) are three cells of the albumen freed from starch to exhibit the pores on their surfaces.

Grains of Paradise (Plate 7, figs. 3, 4, 5) find their legitimate use in the pharmacopœia of the veterinary surgeon, but they have been extensively used to give an artificial strength to spirits, beer, wine, and vinegar —a curious perversion, as it seems to us, of the African's favourite spice, with which he seasons his food. Figure 3 represents a grain magnified six diameters. Its surface is rough, and shining reddish brown, the thin end of the corn being of a pale yellow. The outer coloured skin consists of a series of cells, with curiously undulating walls, highly coloured, which overlie a series of thin-walled long cells placed at a right angle to them. To this succeeds the woody portion of the shell, consisting of very short, double-pointed, channeled cells (*d*), amongst which lie the branched ligneous cells (*e*). Amongst the woody fibres occur the large coloured oil reservoirs, or *cysts*, from which some globules of oil or resinous matter have been expelled.

Datura Stramonium (Plate 7, figs. 6 and 7), the seed of the thorn apple, a native of Greece. It is of the same family as the tobacco plant, and, like it, is highly narcotic in its properties. Its legitimate use is in medicine, administered in very minute doses, either as the dried leaf or powdered grain. Death has resulted from smoking the leaves. The seed, when finely powdered, has been frequently used by desperate characters for *hoccussing* or stupefying the intended victim of a robbery, by surreptitiously adding it to his beer at the public-house bar.

Plate 7, fig. 6, is a grain twice the size of nature; fig. 7 is a diagram, viewed superficially, of the structure of the grain. There is an outer pellicle formed of very thin-walled elongated cells (a), which overlie the coloured skin (b), formed of minute irregular cells with very thick walls. The woody portion (shell) is composed of rows of delicate fibres, placed at right angles to each other (c, d), and amongst these are numerous *cysts* containing colouring matter (e). Two layers of cells (f) enclose the square-shaped cells with very thick walls (g), containing abundance of starch.

Hop-seed (Plate 8, fig. 26), divested of the thin pellicle that covers it, and which is covered with innumerable grains of *Lupulite*, the bitter principle so valuable to the brewer, is a greyish conical seed (Plate 6, fig. 18). We have here only to treat of its structure, which contrasts very curiously with that of those we have been examining.

An exterior layer of thick-walled cells (1) overlies the short double-pointed channeled cells with woody fibres interlacing them (w), which together form the hardened (woody) epiderm of the seed. These form the outer coat (a). Immediately underlying these is a thin, bright, green pellicle, formed of layers of minute cells, with bright green contents (3); these rest upon two sets of elongated cells, one with thick, the other with thin walls (4, 5) ; at right angles to these, as to length, are placed a series of rectangular cells, coloured light brown, which enclose the horny albumen (c 7), containing much oil.

CHAPTER V. (Plates 6, 7.)

HOPS AND YEAST.

The hop, like the barley plant, originally grew wild, and has been brought to its present condition of beauty and fertility, by the care and cultivation which has for years been bestowed upon it, more especially in England. It is classed by botanists amongst a tribe of plants, *Urticaceæ*, taking their name from *Urticadioica* the common stinging-nettle of our hedgerows. Unlike the barley plant, it does not bear what are called perfect flowers, or those which have both stamens and pistil; but these organs are borne by different plants, staminiferous or male, pistiliferous or female.

The seed or nut, when fully ripe, is found at the base of each of the leafy bracts which compose the cones or fruit used by the brewer. These cones are gathered whilst still in a green state, dried on a kiln, and pressed into bags for the market. It is stated that the use of hops in beer was not known until Henry VIII.'s time in 1524, when, the rhyme says,

> "Hops, reformation, bays, and beer,
> Came into England all in one year."

Six years afterwards the same king forbade brewers to put into ale hops and sulphur. In the English laws hops are mentioned for the first time in the fifth year of the reign of Edward VI., that is, in 1552, when some privileges were granted to hop grounds. We may therefore safely presume that they have been carefully cultivated from that time until now, when the best English hops are considered the finest and most delicately flavoured in the world.

The fruit of the plant (technically called *strobilæ*), which is so largely used in brewing, consists of a series of delicate green, semi-transparent bracts, attached to a common stalk (Plate 6, figs. 16, 23), and overlapping at their edges in a very elegant manner.

The seeds (fig. 18) are minute, flattened, conical, berries of a light brown colour; they are attached to the bases of the bracts, which fold over at their lower edges to afford them additional support; and each inner seed-containing bract is covered by another externally (fig. 23). Attached to the outer seed-coat is a beautiful transparent membrane (figs. 19, 24), and on this lie, in countless numbers, minute golden-coloured oval bodies, which are the *Lupulite* so valuable to the brewer. These granules are abundant on the bracts, especially at their bases, where the seed is lodged; they are also present in large quantities on the leaves of the plant (Plate 8, fig. 25).

When one of these granules is placed in water under the microscope, and a drop of sulphuric or nitric acid is added, it immediately bursts, and the coloured matter discharged is seen to consist of excessively minute, somewhat spherical, particles of an oily nature, that move freely and with great rapidity amongst each other with a tremulous motion (Plate 6, fig. 22). This peculiar motion may at times be observed in the contents of the granules before they are broken.

The structure of the bracts is identical with that of the membrane, viz. a layer of oblong cells with thick undulating walls (fig. 24), traversed here and there, where veins occur, with delicate spiral vessels and woody fibres. Minute hairs, with tuberculated surfaces, are also present.

A comman practice amongst hop-buyers is to take a small quantity of the dried hop-fruit, place it in the palm of one hand, and with three or four knuckles of the other to chafe and bruise it. The value of the sample is judged of by the aroma it emits, and the sticky, almost resinous stains left upon the hand. This is a rough but effective way of judging both of the number and produce of the lupulite granules by crushing them. Good sound hops will yield about one-sixth part of their weight of these grains; analysed by the chemist they are found to contain, besides a volatile oil, no fewer than thirteen substances, more or less in combination with each other. But it would appear that to the volatile oil, soluble in water and alcohol, and the bitter principle, *lupulite*, the most valuable properties of the fruit are due.

Knowing from observation how carefully the lupulite granules are lodged on the fruit, I have frequently been at the pains of examining the "spent hops" on the refuse heaps at breweries. I have found a large proportion of the granules perfectly intact, that is to say, not burst, or in any way having yielded their contents; and I may safely affirm that, under the present system adopted at most breweries, of boiling hops without any further separation of the leaves of the fruit than such as is effected by that process, *not more than half their lupulite is made available.* I am not aware that any use has been found for hop leaves, but from the abundance of the lupulite granules on them it is reasonable to presume that, with better knowledge, it will be found that they are not amongst the things which should be thrown aside as useless.

There was at one time an interest of a peculiar kind attaching to the hop plant, one pertaining to the pockets of the British public. Every one has seen, at some time or other, the leaves of roses and other trees swarming with quiet, stupid-looking, green insects, familiar to most under the name of "blight;" but called scientifically plant lice or *aphides.* These creatures have not been objects of my own special study, but I will quote a passage or two relating to them from a most interesting book, "The Letters of Rusticus," by Mr. Newman, which contains an admirable description of these minute creatures, and how, by their formidable depredations, they actually at one time controlled a large share of the national exchequer, at the time when the hop duty was levied.

"To this singular tribe belongs the hop fly, an insect which has more rule over the pockets and tempers of mankind than any other; its abundance or scarcity being almost the only criterion of a scarcity or abundance in the crops of hops; and of all articles of merchandise, the hop is consequently the most variable in price. Owing to the interest taken in the crop of hops, much more close attention has been paid to the hop fly than to any other insect, and you find men conversant with its habits who would blush if you were to suppose them possessed of enough natural history to know the name of the commonest beetle or even bird; but let me assure those that there is nothing derogatory to their manhood, their common sense, or their dignity, in knowing something of the works of nature. I never met with an individual who was the worse man for it. I don't go myself the length of some of your contributors, who measure the joints of an insect's *ears*, as Professor Kennie called them. But perhaps even this is necessary to acquire an accurate knowledge of each kind.

"The hop counties are Kent, Sussex, Surrey, Worcester, and Hereford. The produce of these are termed on the market, Kent, Sussex, Farnham, and Worcester hops. The Farnham are invariably the highest priced, and the Sussex the lowest. The Worcester hops never come on the London market, and have a price of their own which is not much influenced by the general price, as no hops are ever, or very rarely indeed, introduced to supply a deficiency of the Worcester crop should that fail. The hop affords scope for the speculator in two ways: first, the hop itself; secondly, the hop duty. The last is the subject of betting to a very large amount annually.

"The old duty on hops is 10s. 8d. per cent.; the new duty, imposed in 1802, is 12s. 7d., making with the fractions 23s. 4d.; in 1805, 4s. 8d. per cwt. was reduced, so that the actual duty paid is 18s. 8d. per cwt. In betting on the duty the old duty is always understood, and so generally adopted is this mode of expressing the probability of a crop by the betted duty, that the common question is, 'What is the duty laid at?' and as the duty falls the price of hops of course rises, and *vice versâ*. This duty is, however, too much guided by a few men in the Borough, who frequently rise and fall it to answer their own purposes; yet, as the day of picking approaches, the near correspondence of the betted duty and the old duty actually paid is truly surprising. In the year 1802, on the 14th of May, the old duty was laid at £100,000; the fly, however, appearing pretty plentifully towards the end of the month, it sunk to £80,000; the fly increased, and by the end of June the duty had gone down to £60,000; by the end of July to £30,000; by the end of August to £22,000, and by the end of December to £14,000; the duty actually paid this year was £15,463 10s. 5d.

"In 1826 the summer was remarkably dry and hot; we could hardly sleep at night with the sheets on; the thermometer for several nights continued above 70° all the night through; the crop of hops was immense, scarcely a fly was to be found, and the betted duty, which began in May at £120,000, rose to £265,000; the old duty actually paid was £269,331 0s. 9d., the gross duty £468,401 16s. 1d., being the largest amount (until then) ever known. From this it will appear that in duty alone a little insignificant-looking fly has control over £450,000 annual income to the British Treasury; and supposing the hop grounds of England capable of paying this duty annually, which they certainly are, it is very manifest that in 1825 these creatures were the means of robbing the Treasury of £426,000. This seems a large sum, but it is not one-twentieth part of the sums gained and lost by dealers during the year in question.

"The hop fly makes its first appearance generally about the 12th of May, sometimes two days earlier, but almost invariably between the 10th and the 30th; and it is worth noticing that it usually appears on the same day in the four districts of Kent, Sussex, Farnham and Worcester. It always makes its appearance in the winged state. If the weather is warm, with mild, kind rains, during the last twenty days of May these flies begin to produce young ones, which are very small, and are called *deposit*, or *knits*. These grow very fast, and in a few days become green *lice*, which is merely a larger form of the same animal. These lice very soon begin to breed, and so keep on knits and lice, knits and *lice only*, to so great an extent as to destroy the plant, when they appear to die with it. I have never found that the deposit of the hop fly leaves the plant at all, or ever becomes a fly while there; in this respect differing from the aphis of the rose, guelder-rose, bean, &c. Frequently, when the weather in May has been dry and cold and windy, the fly has been known to leave the plant and entirely disappear, even after remaining several days. The direction of the wind has nothing whatever to do with their first appearance; but in a warm westerly wind they will take flight most readily, and be thus distributed.

"You will never find a plant of any kind infested with the aphis, without also observing a number of ants and lady-birds among them, and also a queer-looking insect like a fat lizard, which is, in fact, the caterpillar of the lady-bird. The connexion of the ants and the aphis is of the most peaceful kind that can be conceived: their object is the honey-dew which the aphis emits; and far from hurting the animal which affords them this pleasant food, they show it the greatest possible attention and kindness, licking it all over with their little tongues, and fondling it and patting it and caressing it with their antennæ in the kindest, prettiest way imaginable. Not so the lady-

bird, or its lizard-like caterpillar: these feed on the
'*blights*' most voraciously, a single grub clearing a
leaf, on which were forty or more, in the course of
a day. The perfect lady-bird is a decided enemy to
them, but not so formidable a one as the grub. The
eggs of the lady-bird may often be seen on the hop-
leaf; they are yellow, and five or six in a cluster
placed on their ends: these should on no account
be destroyed (as is too often the case), but, on the
contrary, every encouragement should be given to so
decided a friend to the hop-grower."

Such is Mr. Newman's brief and lucid account of
the hop fly, and after reading it, one cannot feel
surprised that science, applied to the cultivation of
the hop, has not as yet supplied the means of subdu-
ing this troublesome pest. Of late years, the inability
of the hop-growers to pay the duty led to those frequent
interviews with the Chancellor of the Exchequer at the
Treasury for a further instalment of credit for payment
of the duty; which, owing to its variable nature, was
finally abandoned.

YEAST.

According to Pereira, it was only in the year 1835
that the true vegetable nature of yeast was determined,
by a French chemist, Cagniard-Latour. Until his researches were made into the nature of ferments, strong
doubts were entertained whether the plant was not

a microscopic infusorium; although so far back as 1680 the great Leeuwenhoek had both figured and described it as a plant.

If a small portion of fresh yeast is placed on a slip of glass under the microscope, and fed with a moderately strong solution of sugar or saccharine matter, such as fresh worts, it will exhibit a singular appearance. It is composed of a series of cells with minute dots or *nuclei* contained within them, and they are so transparent that the cells can be seen through overlying one another. After being in the brewer's worts an hour or so, these cells begin to germinate by a process of budding. In the course of about three hours the younger cells have attained to the dimensions of their parents, and in about eight hours they begin to form into filaments. At the end of three days they become branched.

Turpin states that in the brewing of 14 butts of beer, in which 35 pounds of dried yeast had been used, 212 pounds of new yeast were produced; in other words, the plants had multiplied to 605 times their original quantity, an astonishing increase for the short period occupied in their production.

There is, however, a difference in the appearance between what is known as *top* yeast and *bottom* yeast, when viewed under the microscope. The former consists of large cells, at the extremities of which small ones are developed; it would, therefore, appear to be produced by a process of budding of individual cells. A temperature of 77° appears to be most favourable to its growth. Bottom yeast does not present this appearance of budding, the cells multiplying most rapidly at a temperature between 32° and 48° F.

Ale yeast is generally considered the best and strongest, and is preferred by bakers. Porter yeast is used in distilleries. There is a very curious fact vouched for by the importers of German and Dutch yeast, and that is that mechanical injury kills or destroys it; it is for this reason imported in bags placed in baskets, and if these be allowed to fall violently on the ground the yeast is spoiled. Yeast thus injured may be distinguished by its dark colour; and from being crumbly or powdery, it becomes soft and glutinous, and sticks to the fingers like flour-paste. Its appearance under the microscope remains unaltered.

When yeast, or the yeast plant, is added to a saccharine solution, such as brewers' worts, a singular and violent action takes place, during which the plant multiplies itself, as we have seen, prodigiously. At the same time, the saccharine matter of the worts becomes decomposed during the growth and multiplication of the plant; and its elements, carbon, hydrogen, and oxygen, re-arrange themselves and become alcohol, carbonic acid gas, and water. This process is known as *fermentation,* and requires simply the addition of yeast to a saccharine solution to produce it.

No very satisfactory solution has yet been arrived at of the exact nature of the forces set in motion by the presence of a plant of the very lowest type of organization when placed in a medium which forms, as it were, its proper food. The chemist can evolve carbonic acid gas from marble, and he can produce water by the combination of its elements, hydrogen and oxygen; but by no process yet known can he combine carbon and hydrogen with oxygen, in proportions to produce alcohol, excepting by the agency of the yeast plant placed in a saccharine solution.

CHAPTER VI.

MALT, BEER, SPIRIT.

Setting aside skill in process of manufacture, malt, beer, and spirits depend for their production mainly on the exertion of the vital forces with which barley and other seeds are endowed, and the peculiar properties of the yeast plant.

I have before spoken of the wonderful vigour exhibited by barley seeds when placed in favourable circumstances. Indeed, we have only to steep the grain in cold water for a few hours to convince ourselves of the change this simple medium is enabled to exert upon it in a short time. The maltster, in converting barley into malt, strives to imitate as closely as possible the natural growth of the seed when placed in soil, and for this purpose he has to supply it with moisture and a certain degree of warmth. The first of these objects is attained by steeping the grain in cold water for about fifty hours, changing the water once during this interval. At the completion of this stage of the process the grain is found to have lost its light colour, to have swollen considerably, and to have become comparatively soft.

The water is next drained from the grain, which is now removed to a four-sided rectangular frame (for the purpose of being charged with duty by the revenue officers) to a depth varying from ten to thirty inches. From this frame it is removed in a few hours to the working floor (a level surface of slate, tiles, or stucco), and laid thick and close so as to preserve the heat evolved by germination, which has now actively commenced. Small white pips will, in a few days, make their appearance at one end of the grain, whilst on its back a raised protuberance underlying the husk will be seen lengthening itself from day to day.

It is now the maltster's special care, by turning the grain on the floor, spreading it thickly or thinly, to regulate its temperature, so as to obtain a thoroughly even growth throughout the floor, a result which is made more certain of attainment by sprinkling the grain with water. When the rootlets extend beyond the grain some half an inch in length, and the plumule extends to about three-fourths of its length (Plate 2, fig. 2) the germination or growth of the grain may be considered sufficiently advanced, and at this stage is arrested by throwing it into a chamber of hot air provided with a tiled floor, perforated with minute holes. The heat of this chamber (the kiln) is maintained by a fire of charcoal, wood, or coke, placed underneath, and is gradually raised as the water escapes from the grain as steam, which finds its way through the roof, usually furnished with a wooden dome, which turns with the wind. In proportion to the briskness of the kiln fire, and the skill with which the grain has been turned during this process of drying, will much of the value of the malt depend.

Pale malt is generally dried at a temperature of 140° to 150° F. The darker kinds, used for highly coloured beer and porter, are known as "*amber*" malt, and "*snapped*" malt, these being obtained by drying at a temperature varying from 185° to 210° F. To produce the latter description of malt the kiln fire is fed with wood only (dry oak or elm being preferred for this purpose), and by increasing the draught of the kiln fire, the flames are made to reach the perforated tiles on which the malt rests. Whilst thus heated, the malt is laid very thin and kept continually stirred by the workmen, and as each grain becomes gradually scorched, the husk bursts with a snapping noise; hence its name. Roasted malt is prepared by roasting the paler descriptions of malt in cylinders before a strong fire, until it becomes black. In this condition it is used merely for giving a dark colour to porter and stout.

In the manufacture of *patent* or crystallized malt, barley of inferior quality is generally used, and the process of malting it is conducted in the same way as for making ordinary malt, excepting that the grain, whilst working on the floor, is more plentifully supplied with water, and the germination of the grain is carried to a greater extent, the process being continued until the future stem extends the whole length of the grain. In some cases it is allowed to grow until it bursts the husk, and extends to the length of half an inch or more beyond it.

The drying apparatus consists of an oven, having closely fitted iron doors. This contains an iron cylinder covered with wire gauze, which is fixed in the oven and so arranged that it can be readily withdrawn for filling or emptying. A rotatory motion is given to the cylinder by means of machinery, and it is so placed that, when at rest, one side of it is exposed to the action of a coke fire placed at one side of the oven. The process of drying consists in charging the cylinder with the germinated barley, allowing ample space for the free motion of the grains; it is then made to rotate on its axis slowly, so that every part of its surface becomes in turn exposed to the action of the fire. The process of drying occupies about three hours, and when successfully conducted the grain is found to have increased in size, and to have assumed a beautiful amber colour; internally the contents have become highly crystalline in structure, possessing a remarkably sweet, aromatic taste. Brewers have found patent malt a valuable addition when used in small quantities with ordinary malt.

Competent authorities state that during the conversion of barley into malt one-fifth of its original weight, or twenty per cent., is lost. Of this two per cent. is dissolved out in the process of steeping the grain, two per cent. more is given off during the early stages of fermentation in the form of carbonic acid gas. In the process of kiln-drying four per cent. loss occurs by the death and falling away of the rootlets, and twelve per cent. more by the evaporation of the moisture which the grain has absorbed. A good sample of barley skilfully worked in malting will yield an increase in bulk of about five per cent.

In outward appearance malt differs from barley in the greater fulness of the grains, and by the appearance of a "bloom" upon their outer husks, which replaces the brighter golden hue observable on the grains of barley before being steeped in water. Internally the contents of malt grains should be extremely white and friable, and possess an almost aromatic sweetness; and the ends through which the rootlets once protruded will be found to be distinctly perforated.

The changes brought about in the conversion of barley into malt are best exemplified when malt is crushed and submitted to the action of hot water by the brewer or distiller. Then, instead of the turbid, milky solution which crushed barley yields by this treatment, we have a transparent and sweet solution, perfectly palatable; and it is of this solution, technically called "worts," that the brewer and distiller manufacture "our strong drink."

A peculiar principle, called *diastase*, is evolved in the

process of malting barley, and on its production much of the value of malt depends. A part of the starch which barley contains is converted, by the influence of the *diastase*, into grape sugar. And when brought into contact with the meal of other grain, such as oats, &c., in the presence of hot water, diastase has the power of converting the starch of the raw grain also into grape sugar, and it thus saccharizes, or sweetens, the whole mass.

In the manufacture of beer the use of raw grain is prohibited by law, but the brewer obtains his worts, as they are called, by bruising the malt, adding to it hot water at 150° to 180° F., whilst stirring the mixture. To this solution when cold he adds the hops, either in infusion or as they come from the grower, concentrates the whole mixture by boiling, and when sufficiently cooled he adds the yeast as a ferment, and when fermentation has proceeded to a given point he checks it.

The distiller places both crushed malt and crushed grain (oats most frequently) in his mash tun, adds warm water, and keeps the whole thoroughly stirred. When the wort so obtained has sufficiently cooled, which requires to be rapidly done, he dispenses with hops, but adds yeast as a ferment. This fermentation he drives to its utmost limit,—his endeavour being to convert all the saccharine matter of the wort into alcohol, and this alcohol is separated from the wash as it is called by distillation, a process now to be briefly described.

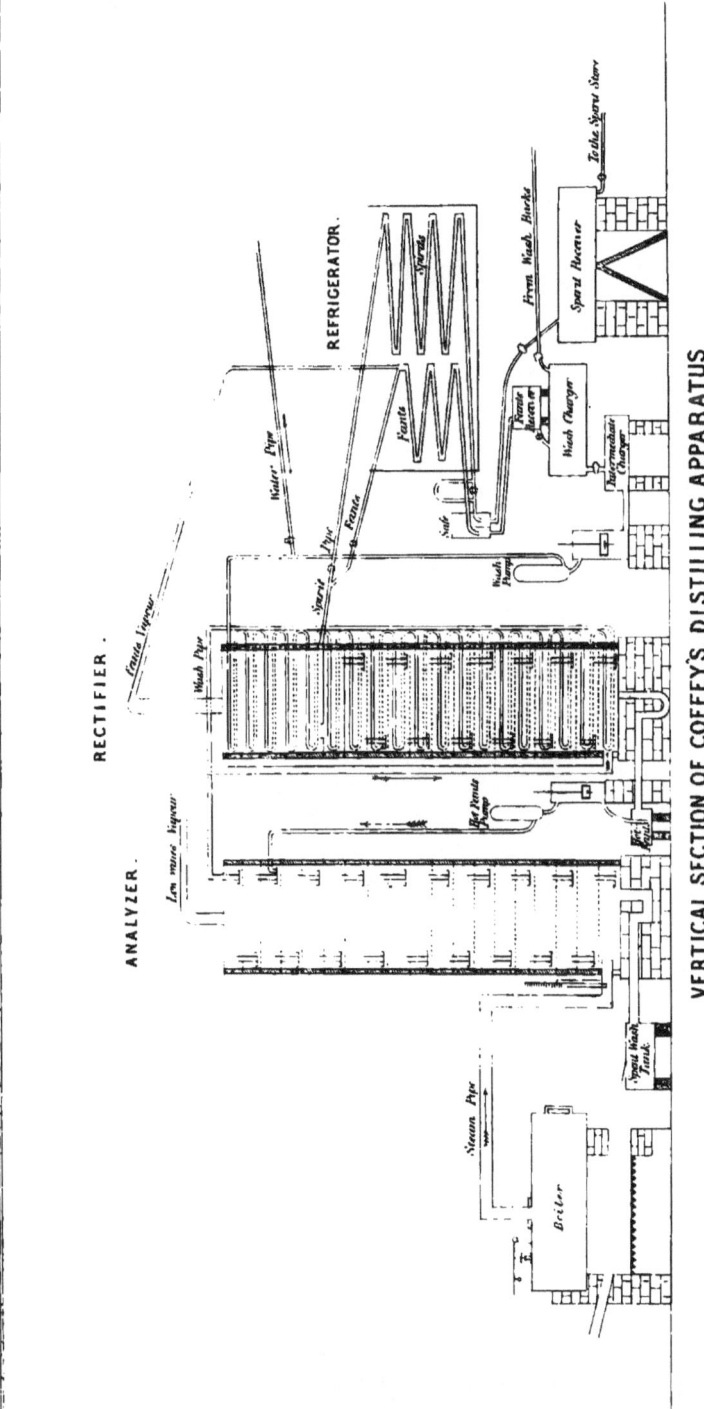

VERTICAL SECTION OF COFFEY'S DISTILLING APPARATUS
WITH THE PRINCIPAL PIPES & VESSELS CONNECTED THEREWITH.

DISTILLATION.

The ordinary method of distilling Distillers' Wash, and the only one formerly practised, is by boiling it in a closely-covered copper vessel, the head of which is attached to a pipe of considerable length, surrounded by cold water. In this pipe the impure vapour of spirit, called "Low Wines," is condensed in a receiver, and again subjected to the same process to extract the pure spirit. By this process there are four different products obtained by two distillations: in the first, a very impure spirit distils over, known as Low Wines, which has a most nauseous smell and taste. After being collected in a receiver, this is again distilled, the product being a tolerably pure spirit and an essential oil, called Feints; and a fourth product, in not very abundant quantity, Fusel oil.

Of late years the practice of distilling by steam with "Coffey's Apparatus" has become very common; it is a very interesting process, and will be easily understood on reference to the illustration. The apparatus consists essentially of two large upright wooden or iron boxes, divided at intervals into compartments by a series of perforated copper plates (represented by the dotted lines), called the *Analyser* and the *Rectifier*. Each plate of the analyser is, in addition, furnished with a pipe (p), inserted into it and rising a few inches above its surface; the other end of it dips into a shallow cup (c) on the plate beneath.

The rectifier is similarly furnished with dipping pipes and cups; but, in addition to these, a closed metal pipe of great length is inserted continuously between every compartment by being bent upon itself as it enters each of them.

The wash being in readiness, and the steam in the boiler in sufficient quantity to work at a pressure of from 6 to 7 lbs. to the square inch, the wash is forced, by means of a pump, into the pipe which leads from the *intermediate wash charger* to the top of the rectifier, in the direction of the arrow. It passes through this pipe for its entire length, and through each bend of it, until it at length reaches the top of the analyser, on to which it is discharged. When it has fallen on this plate in sufficient quantity to fill the cup, and has risen to the height of the orifice of the *dipping pipe*, it flows through this to the plate beneath, and so on in succession downwards from plate to plate.

Whilst the flow of wash is thus proceeding in one direction through the metal pipe, steam is let in at the bottom of the analyser, and rises through each perforated plate. Coming in contact with the wash which is on it, the steam combines with the impure spirit of the wash (low wines vapour), and conveys it through the pipe at the top of the analyser down to the bottom of the *rectifier*. Here, in rising, it meets with the surfaces of the pipe containing the descending wash, and as these surfaces are necessarily coldest at the top (because there exposed less to the heating effect of the rising vapour), they act as more powerful condensers than the lower ones in separating the vapour of water from the spirit and the feints. So much of the spirit and feints vapours as are not condensed at the plate to which the spirit pipe is attached are so either at the top of the rectifier from which they fall to the spirit plate, or else pass on as vapour to the refrigerator, where they are condensed into the liquid state and collected in separate vessels. Whilst the process is going on, the feints fall from plate to plate of the rectifier in a condensed state, and are collected through a syphon pipe passing from the bottom of the rectifier to the hot feints receiver. From this vessel they are pumped up through a pipe and discharged nearly on to the top plate of the analyser, and are redistilled from the down-flowing wash, with which they mix. As the wash in the analyser becomes deprived of its spirit, or "spent" as it is called, it passes to the spent-wash tank, from which it is delivered to be used as a useful drink for cows and pigs.

The real merits of this very ingenious contrivance are a saving of time, labour, and fuel, and in addition a more complete separation of the spirit from its impurities and from water. The time and labour attached to a second distillation (the low wines), as in the ordinary still, are both saved, the comparatively low temperature of the wash in the rectifier acts as a refrigerator on the spirit and feints vapours, whilst, on the other hand, the heat of this vapour in the analyser warms the descending wash, and causes it more readily to part with its spirit.

It has the additional merit of separating the spirit from the wash more effectually than by the common method. This is due to the fact that all the wash is brought into contact with the steam in the analyser, and such of the products as are condensed in the rectifier, as "*hot feints,*" are again subject to the action of the steam.

Coffey's apparatus is capable of producing spirit with only four and a half per cent. of water mixed with it; and when in good working order can exhaust from two to three thousand gallons of wash per hour, producing a spirit of a uniform strength, ranging from sixty-five to sixty-seven per cent. over-proof.

Mr. Young, of the Inland Revenue, states that "the quantity of spirits which may be produced from the several materials used by distillers depends very much upon the quality of the respective materials; but it may be assumed that, on an average,—

1 quarter of	Barley Malt	will yield	18	gallons at proof.	
1 "	Malt and Grain	"	20	"	
1 cwt. of	Sugar	"	10	"	
1 "	Molasses	"	7	"	
1 "	Rice	"	$7\frac{1}{2}$	"	
1 ton of	Beetroot	"	15	"	

Proof spirit is merely an arbitrary standard of strength, adopted by the Legislature in laying the duty. It means that distilled water at 51° Fahrenheit being considered as unity, an equal measure of proof spirit shall weigh twelve-thirteenths of such water.

The following table will show the quantities of spirit in gallons, at proof, which have been manufactured in the United Kingdom in each year for the last ten years.

Scotch and Irish whiskies, whether made from pure malt, or malt and grain, are the direct product of distilled wash, with water added to decrease their strength. English spirit of similar manufacture is generally used for rectifying or redistilling with *juniper* berries, *carraway* and other seeds, for the production of gin, or for compounding with various ingredients in the manufacture of British brandy and cordials.

SPIRITS.

Accounts for the Ten Years ended 31st March, 1866.

Year ended 31st March.	Quantities of Spirit made in				Quantities of Spirits consumed as Beverage, and Rates of Duty on the same, in							Year ended 31st March.
	England.	Scotland.	Ireland.	United Kingdom.	England.		Scotland.		Ireland.		United Kingdom.	
	Gallons.	Gallons.	Gallons.	Gallons.	Gallons.	Rates of Duty per Gallon.	Gallons.	Rates of Duty per Gallon.	Gallons.	Rates of Duty per Gallon.	Gallons.	
						s. d.		s. d.		s. d.		
1857	8,318,895	12,159,615	8,910,637	29,089,147	11,386,279	8 0	5,368,052	8 0	6,807,412	6 2	23,561,743	1857
1858	8,228,134	13,349,527	9,857,107	31,434,768	11,634,198	,,	5,575,171	,,	6,783,207	{ 6 2 / 8 0 }	23,992,480	1858
1859	6,784,263	12,747,615	7,670,801	27,202,679	11,860,196	,,	5,324,875	,,	5,418,409	8 0	22,603,480	1859
1860	7,597,763	13,312,365	7,105,593	28,315,721	12,904,029	{ 8 0 / 8 6 / 10 0 }	5,581,173	{ 8 0 / 8 1 / 10 0 }	5,950,241	{ 8 0 / 8 1 / 10 0 }	26,435,443	1860
1861	7,911,822	11,211,648	4,801,115	23,924,585	11,198,113	10 0	4,250,265	10 0	4,191,560	10 0	19,639,938	1861
1862	7,852,710	12,545,904	4,404,006	24,802,620	10,728,412	,,	4,416,596	,,	4,190,128	,,	19,335,136	1862
1863	7,634,524	13,187,661	4,137,544	24,959,729	10,481,577	,,	4,511,193	,,	3,891,759	,,	18,884,529	1863
1864	7,947,167	13,712,154	4,501,551	26,160,872	10,720,768	,,	4,769,150	,,	3,933,526	,,	19,423,444	1864
1865	7,806,102	14,502,089	5,483,208	27,792,299	11,196,524	,,	5,029,610	,,	4,157,241	,,	20,383,375	1865
1866	7,426,243	13,097,101	5,746,680	26,270,024	11,257,505	,,	5,202,714	,,	4,518,254	,,	20,978,473	1866

CHAPTER VII.

TOBACCO AND SOME OTHER LEAVES.

IF the reader has mastered the detail of the foregoing chapters, he will find what follows of some use, should he care to analyse for himself the tobacco which he smokes or chews, or the snuff which he uses.

Most of the tobacco leaves imported into this country arrive packed in large hogsheads, in which after packing they are submitted to an enormous pressure. They rarely suffer any injury in this process, and for purposes of microscopic analysis are, after steeping in water, nearly as useful as if green and freshly plucked. Comparing the margins of any tobacco leaves with those of other plants we shall find them *entire*, that is, even and unbroken (Plate 9, fig. 1), unlike the borders of other leaves cut into toothed notches, or into rounded segments, or into larger segments like the dandelion leaf. American, German, Dutch, and most of the tobacco leaves of commerce are without stalks, being attached to the stem of the plant by the midrib, or large central vein; and this is a very marked character which they possess. So that if we found in our cigar a portion of a leaf, either possessing a stalk or a divided margin, we should safely conclude that we had alighted upon an adulteration.

Moreover, the midrib of tobacco in section presents (as in "bird's-eye" cut tobacco) a horse-shoe form (Plate 9, fig. 5), in which the *woody* or *fibrous* tissue lies as a central mass, surrounded by the cellular tissue. In this latter character it closely resembles foxglove (Plate 10, fig. 5), but this last differs from it in the *woody* tissue being curved upwards at the ends, and the margin of the section, more particularly on its upper surface, having strong and decided curves.

In all the leaves with which tobacco is, or is likely to be adulterated, the woody tissues of their midribs, or stalks, lie in separate detached bundles, as will be readily seen on comparing Plate 9, figs. 8 and 11, and Plate 10, figs. 2, 5, and 8, with Plate 9, fig. 5.

The forms of the leaves of dock (Plate 9, fig. 9), burdock (Plate 9, fig. 6), chicory (Plate 10, fig. 1), foxglove, and comfrey (Plate 10, fig. 4), with the transverse-vertical sections of their midribs, are given in Plates 9 and 10. The peculiar characters of the leaves will be evident on inspection; those of the sections of the midribs consisting of differences in the forms of their outlines, whether plain, more or less grooved or lobed, and the general form and distribution of the woody tissues of each amongst the cellular tissue.

Compare, for instance, the forms of the leaves of

burdock and dock (plants growing wild nearly everywhere in Britain, and to be had for the plucking), or either of these, again, with comfrey; and all three with the tobacco leaf. Observe the forms of their bases, points, and margins, and the characteristic distinctions of them will be immediately apparent.

Take a portion of the midrib of each leaf, and cut a very thin slice of it at a right angle to its length, and compare them with each other under the microscope with an object glass of low power. The differences of these will be seen in the general forms of their outlines, whether plain, grooved, or lobed, and the shape and distribution of the *woody* amongst the *cellular* tissues. Notice, more especially, the general outlines and upper surfaces of the midrib sections of *dock* (Plate 9, fig. 11), and *burdock* (Plate 9, fig. 8), and the marked characters which distinguish them from that of *tobacco* (Plate 9, fig. 5) or *comfrey* (Plate 10, fig. 5). Those of *chicory* (Plate 10, fig. 2) and *foxglove* are as decidedly marked.

Carrying our analyses still further, by adding greater power to the microscope, our leaves furnish us with invaluable and infallible evidence in the minute hairs with which their surfaces are clothed, and which, from their delicacy and pliability, elude the grinding action of the snuff-mill. These hairs are attached to, and grow on the skins of the upper and under surfaces of leaves, their midribs and veins, lying scattered in greater or less abundance amongst the *stomates* or breathing-pores of these parts. The tobacco leaf is furnished with two forms of hairs, long and short. The former are composed of three or four elongated cells, joined end to end, the whole surmounted by a cluster of minute cells, forming a *gland* which contains a rich brown colouring matter. These are called *glandular* hairs, and they have a pair, sometimes more, cells forming a compound base. The short hairs are unicellular, with a cluster of cells at one end, also containing colouring matter. I call these hairs club-shaped; their bases are simple (Plate 9, figs. 2, 3, 4).

The leaves of *dock* are furnished with peculiar club-shaped unicellular hairs, free from colouring matter, but having their surfaces marked with peculiar wavy lines (striated), formed by a wrinkling, as it were, of thin cell walls (Plate 9, fig. 10). This is a very marked feature of them; equally so is the presence on the skin of the blade, or thin portion of the leaf, of numerous circular cavities (*glands*), composed of clusters of cells built into the substance of the leaf, forming minute chambers containing crystals of oxalate of lime (raphides) (Plate 9, fig. 12). The hairs described are found mostly on the midribs and veins of the leaves, the *glands* on the leaf-blades.

Leaves of the *burdock* plant are covered on their under surfaces with a dense, greenish-white, woolly substance. When a minute portion of the skin to which this is attached is separated from the leaf, this woolliness is resolved by the microscope into a mass of very beautiful transparent hairs, each composed of a string, or bead, of square-shaped cells, joined together; these gradually diminish in size towards the end of the hair, which terminates in a slender, transparent filament of very great length. The bases of these hairs are compound (Plate 9, fig. 7).

The leaves of the *chicory* plant have a peculiar interest in connexion with the subject of tobacco adulteration. Some years ago, tons of these leaves steeped in tar oil were seized in Ireland by the revenue officers on the premises of a cigar maker, by whom they had been freely used as "*fillers*" for pure Havannahs, and so good was the sophistication, that many practical men were actually deceived by them. When the leaves were unrolled their margins (Plate 10, fig. 1) at once told a tale, and when their skins were stripped and examined under the microscope they told another, for attached to them were discovered an abundance of minute hairs, as unlike those on the tobacco leaf as could be well imagined. For about a third of its length each hair is composed of a number of oblong cells, laid side to side, and end to end; these gradually lessen in number until they form a row of single cells joined together, the hair being finished by a single cell, curiously curved. A cluster of cells form a compound base to each hair (Plate 10, fig. 3).

Among the simplest forms of hairs are those which form the peculiar down on the under surfaces of *foxglove* leaves. They are simple filaments of single oblong cells, joined end to end, ending occasionally with a single oval cell, perfectly colourless, but more frequently with one that is slightly curved, like that of chicory. It is, however, readily distinguished from that hair by the form and structure at its base and lower series of cells; but, like it, the *foxglove* hair has a compound base.

Another of our wild plants, *comfrey* (Plate 10, fig. 6), found growing on hedge-banks and in marshy places, is furnished with two forms of hair, both of them very singular in their appearance. On this leaf are a profusion of unicellular hairs, with compound bases, and very sharp points, the whole surface of the hair being wrinkled or striated (as we found in *dock* but much more coarsely). This is the first instance we have seen of a single-celled hair with a compound base, which in this instance is very prominent. The length and sharp point of this hair readily distinguish it from the club-shaped ones of *dock*. The second form of hair on comfrey leaf is also single-celled and curved, ending in a sharp point, which gives it a form somewhat resembling a fish-hook. The surfaces of these hairs are not striated, and their bases are simple.

The leaf of the Jerusalem artichoke furnishes in abundance examples of beautiful compound hairs with recurved points and compound bases; their surfaces being covered with minute warts (Plate 10, fig. 9). The student may usefully compare the horizontal section of the midrib of this leaf; first, with that of chicory, which it most resembles, and, next with those previously illustrated. I think it will be difficult to find amongst natural objects better examples of exquisite gradations of form and structure than these wayside weeds do furnish.

For the purpose of studying the forms and characters of these hairs under the microscope, the epidermis, or skin of the leaf is detached from the main rib of veins on the under side of the leaf by gently cutting it with a very sharp knife-blade, raising the edge of the skin with a pair of delicate forceps, and peeling it off in a lateral direction. Or, if the skin of the leaf-blade is required, by making a slight incision at that point where the blade joins a vein or midrib. The delicate membrane thus obtained is carefully placed in water on a glass slide covered with thin glass, and, if necessary, a drop of caustic potash added to the water by means of a glass rod to remove impurities.

To examine the structure internally, a piece of it is inserted between two pieces of cork; these are then placed face to face and inserted into the mouth of a glass tube. After moistening the cork with water, thin, transverse, vertical sections may be obtained by using a very sharp razor, or, what is better, one of the fine knives used by surgeons in delicate dissections and operations on the eye.

Sections thus obtained will resemble, according to their thickness, the loosely aggregated cells of the tobacco leaf (Plate 9, fig. 4), or those more compactly arranged, as in the leaf of the hop.

In both these sections the cells containing green colouring matter, the intercellular cavities of the leaf, the external stomates, and the epidermis with hairs attached, are well seen.

Snuff, whether *moist* or *high dried*, should consist of nothing but the tobacco leaves (with or without midribs) in a fairly divided state, being reduced to powder after undergoing the processes of fermentation, and, in the manufacture of high-dried snuff, of roasting.

Starches of the cereals, pea-meal, bran, sawdust of various woods, malt rootlets, fustic, oxides of iron and lead, and ground glass, have formed at various times favourite adulterations with unprincipled tradesmen. In a certain part of Ireland, which shall be nameless, the acorn-cup of a large species of oak, Valonia, growing on the shores of the Mediterranean, have been extensively used in the adulteration of high-dried snuff. It need not be supposed that they were introduced into the country solely for this purpose, their proper application being in the tanner's pit, where they are very valuable. On the principle, I presume, that they would form a difficult ingredient to find a name for, even with a powerful microscope, they were freely used for a time, until detection and punishment put an end to the speculation. I have given a figure of the microscopic structure of the Valonia acorn-cup at Plate 8, fig. 27, and of the hairs with which it is covered externally. It partakes largely of the peculiar characters which distinguish the structure of our fruit-stones, and like them, contains an abundance of very thick walled, porous cells, lying scattered or in masses amongst cellular tissue. No such cells as these exist anywhere in the tobacco leaf or plant, and they are so characteristic as to proclaim at once their nature, if not their exact origin. The hairs are simple hollow filaments, and are occasionally branched.

It is unnecessary, even if space permitted, to allude further to snuff adulterations. It is sufficient to have named them for the purpose of showing the student in what direction to look for the purpose of observing and detecting them.

Any student wishing to gain an elementary knowledge of plant structure, cannot, I think, do better than follow me in this analysis of "Our Strong Drink and Tobacco Smoke."

DESCRIPTIONS OF PLATES.

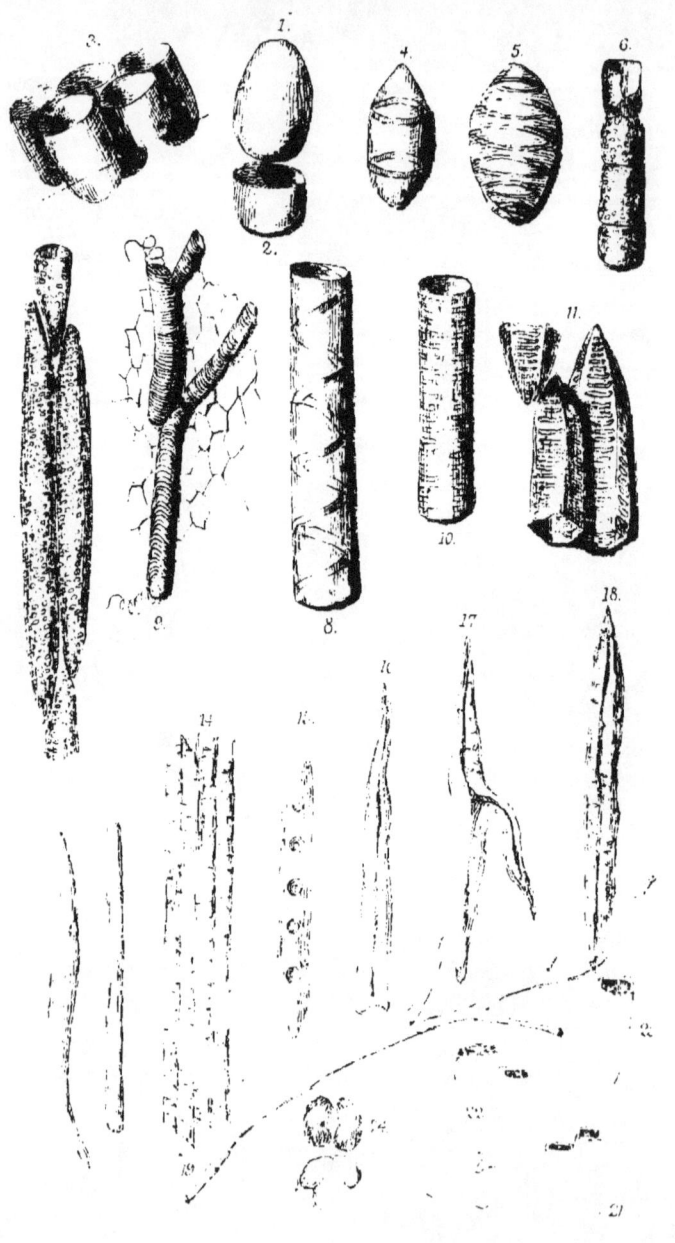

PLATE I.

FIG.
1. A representation in miniature of an inflated sheep bladder.
2. Part of same cut across its length.
3. A collection of same supposed to be held together.
4. A vegetable cell with two rings formed in its interior.
5. Another, with six rings.
6. Four cells super-imposed, united to form a tube.
7. Dotted ducts.
8. A vegetable vessel with deposit formed on its interior in a spiral curve.
9. Spiral vessels from leaf veins.
10. A reticulated vessel.
11. A scalariform duct.
12. A double-pointed wood cell.
13. A square-ended wood cell.
14. A collection of same as *tissue*.
15. A pitted cell from a deal shaving.
16. A part of a single-pointed wood fibre.
17. A branched wood fibre.
18. A pointed ditto.
19. A branched fibre from woody portion of a seed-coat.
20. An oblong cell from skin of leaf.
21. Two irregularly-shaped cells from skin of leaf.
22. Two irregularly-shaped cells from the skin of *Cocculus Indicus*.
23. A cell with wavy outline, from skin of leaf, under side.
24. Kidney-shaped cells from skin of leaf forming a *stoma*.
25. Same viewed in vertical section.

PLATE II.

FIG.
1. A grain of Barley n.s. with the husks removed from lower end to show *the embryo*.
2 to 8. Grains of barley in different stages of development (growth) when placed in moist earth: 4 to 16 days.
9. A diagram of the young barley plant.
10. A young rootlet greatly magnified, showing the *cap* or *sucker*.
11. A young newly-formed leaf with *strap*, *s*.
12. A portion of a fully-developed leaf of barley: *s*, stalk, *st*, strap, *b*, blade.
13. A minute portion of a leaf blade cut transverse-vertically and highly magnified, showing the position of the parallel veins (*v*) of the leaf.
14. A horizontal section of barley stem (straw), highly magnified. The inner circle represents a section of the growing point of stem, wood bundles in both.
15. A vertical section of the same.
16. A minute portion of skin of young straw with *hairs* developing, highly magnified.

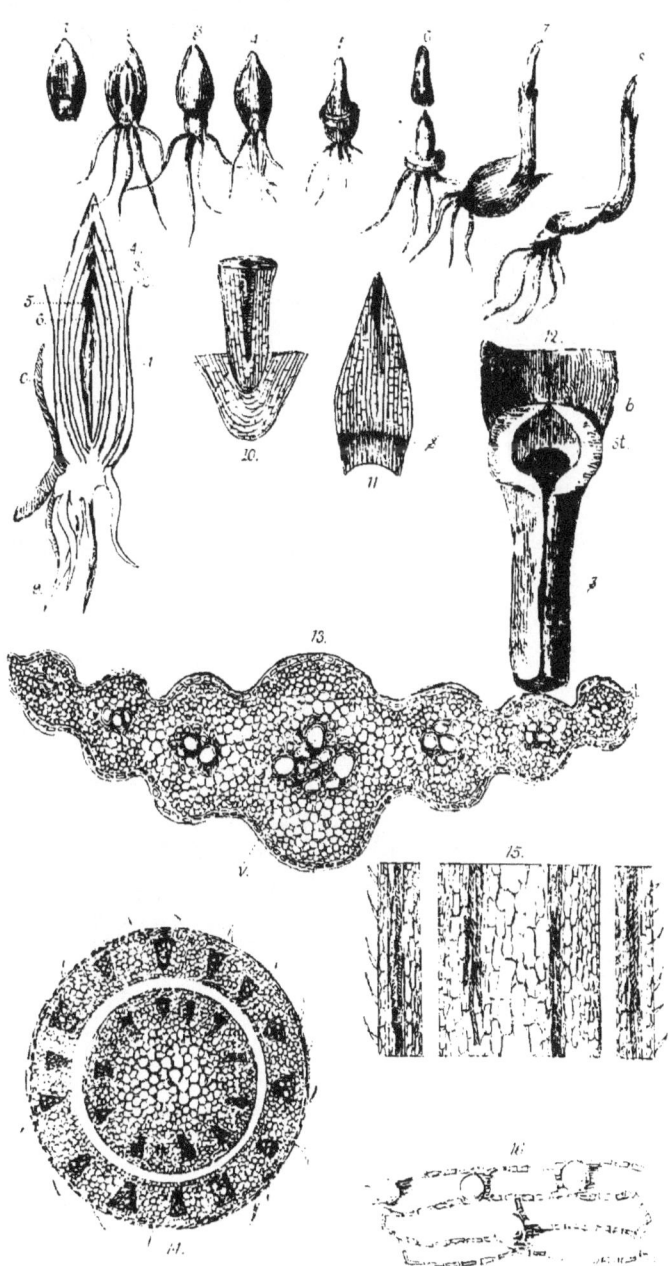

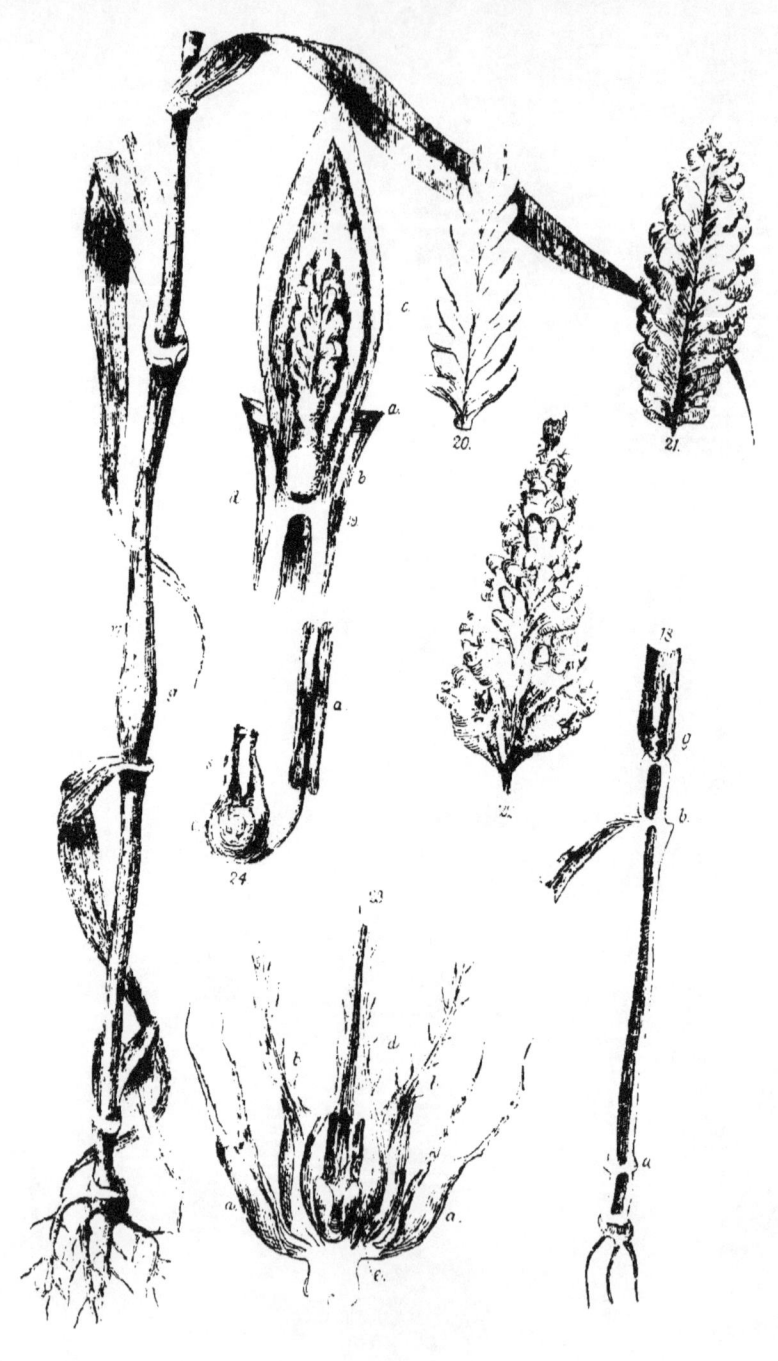

PLATE III.

FIG.
17. A barley plant, n. s. : *g*, swelling caused by contained *inflorescence*.
18. Part of same divided down the centre, showing the size and position of *inflorescence* (*g*) : *a*, and *b*, nodes of the stem.
19. The same highly magnified, showing the divisions of the *inflorescence* into undeveloped (*a*), and developing (*c*) portions : these last will form the future flowers. *b* is the growing point of the stem just separated from the last-formed node.
20. *Inflorescence* in a very rudimentary condition, highly magnified.
21. Further development of same into lobed masses.
22. More advanced *inflorescence :* in which the lobes are seen forming divisions amongst themselves.
23. One of the lobes developed into a perfect flower : *c*, stem, *a a*, lateral florets, *b b d* outer, and *c* inner coats of flower.
24. Ovary (*o*) and one stamen (*a*), separated : *s*, styles with feathery stigmas, on which a pollen granule has fallen.

PLATE IV.

FIG.
25. A vertical section of mature barley straw, highly magnified, showing the dark woody bundles of spiral and other vessels amongst the elongated fibrous cells. The central portion (pith) is not renewed, the stem therefore becomes hollow.
26. A portion of *silicated* epidermis or skin from mature stem, showing the curved prickly hairs, highly magnified.
27. A portion of the epidermis of a leaf without hairs.
28. A minute portion of a very young awn, with spiral vessels (*v*), and (*h*) young hairs developing.
29. A diagram showing the position of the inflorescence relatively to the surrounding leaves: *a*, the oldest leaf; *b c*, those next formed.
30. Portion of (*e*) barley ear, showing the lateral supports (*ss*) by which each grain is protected.
31. *Pollen granules*, enormously magnified.

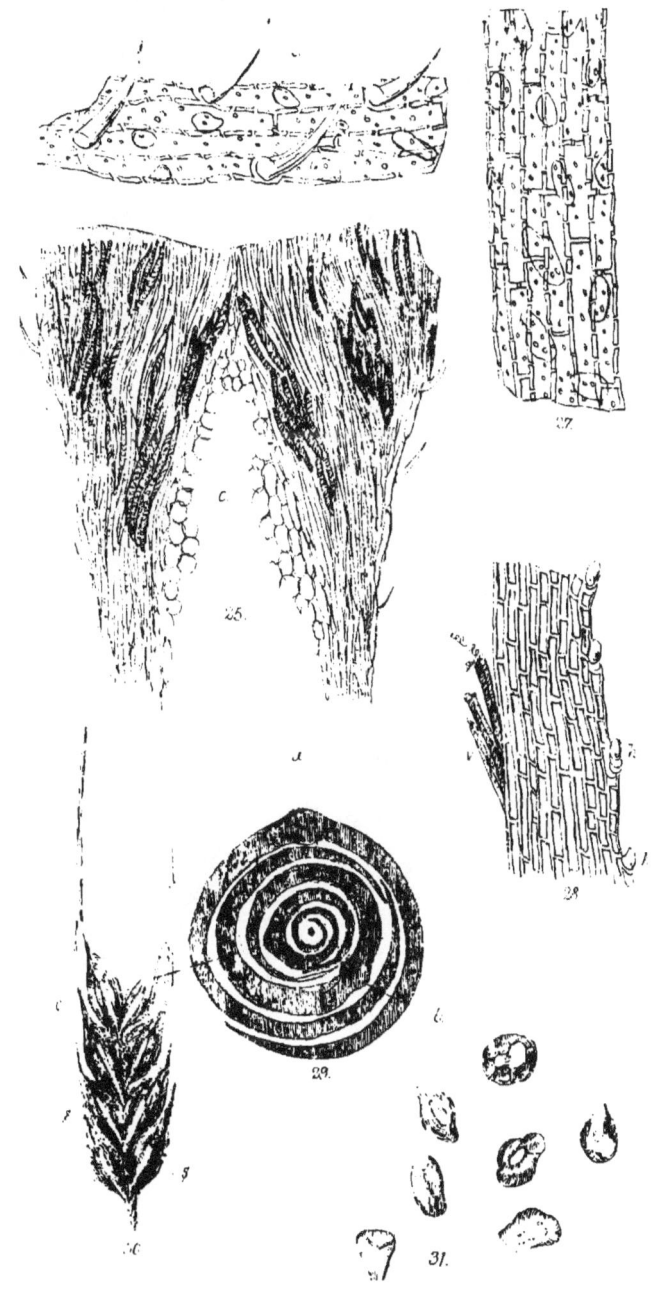

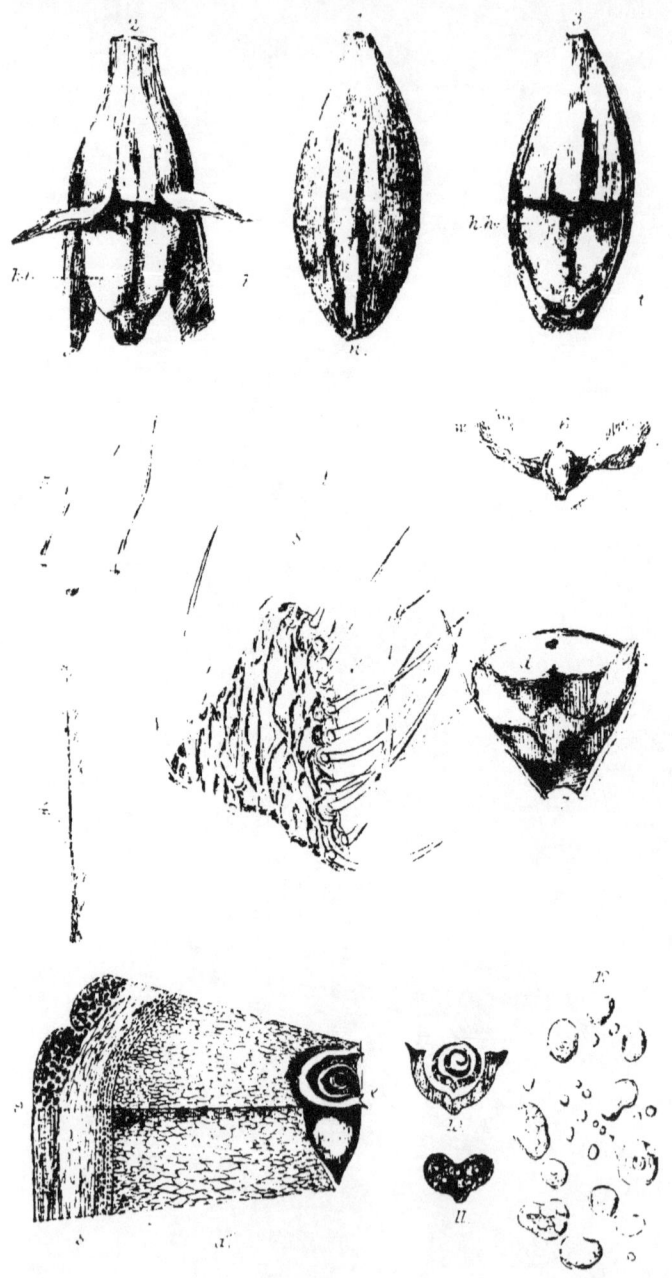

PLATE V.

FIG.
1. A grain of barley greatly magnified, showing the small hard body *n*—the *needle*—at the base of the grain covering the folds of the outer skin.
2. Another (damaged) grain. The outer seed-coat (*h*) has been raised to show the manner in which it separates with force, the central portion being cut away; *hh*, is the inner coat. The "needle" in this specimen was wanting.
3. Another (perfect) grain, in which is present a peculiar minute body overlying the inner coat—*the tuft, t*: *h* and *h h* as in previous figure.
4. The *needle*, greatly magnified.
5. Hard silicated hairs from its borders, highly magnified.
6. *The tuft* removed from base of grain : *ww*, wings ; *s*, spongiole.
7. The position of the tuft (*t*) relatively to the embryo (*c*) when the grain is cut across: *a*, albumen of the seed ; *hh*, outer seed-coat.
8. A minute portion of wing of tuft highly magnified, showing the cellular tissue to which the long delicate filaments are attached.
9. Section of seed through the embryo (*c*), highly magnified: *s*, seed-coats ; *a*, albumen deprived of starch.
10. Horizontal section of upper or leaf portion of embryo.
11. Ditto, of portion forming rootlets.
12. Starch granules from albumen of seed, greatly magnified.

PLATE VI.

FIG.
13. Seed coats of barley seeds. *a*, the outer one formed of three layers of cells: 1. the tabular silicated cells of the epiderm; 2. the elongated fibrous cells underlying these; 3. the tabular thick-walled cells lying across and under these. *b*, the inner coat, consisting of, 4. a delicate pellicle formed of long very thin-walled cells, overlying four or five rows of cells; 5. with thick walls containing brown colouring matter. 6. *c*, large albumen cells loaded with starch granules.
14. Silica plates on outer layer of cells of skin when dry, highly magnified.
15. The same after the grain has been steeped in water for some time. The dark lines show the separation of the plates owing to the distension of the grain.
16. A *strobile* or fruit of the Hop, n. s.
17. A bract of same highly magnified, showing the position of—
18. The seed at its base, n.s.
19. Seed with investing membrane highly magnified to show the *lupulite*, very abundant on this membrane.
20, 21. Seed divested of membrane viewed in face and on edge.
22. A granule of *lupulite* burst with dilute sulphuric acid.
23. A portion of a fruit of brewer's spent-hops, showing the position of the seeds and lupulite grains unaffected by boiling.
24. A minute portion of the seed pellicle or base of bract (17), beset with lupulite: *s v*, spiral vessels and fibre; *h*, hairs; *c*, cellular tissue in layer, largely magnified.

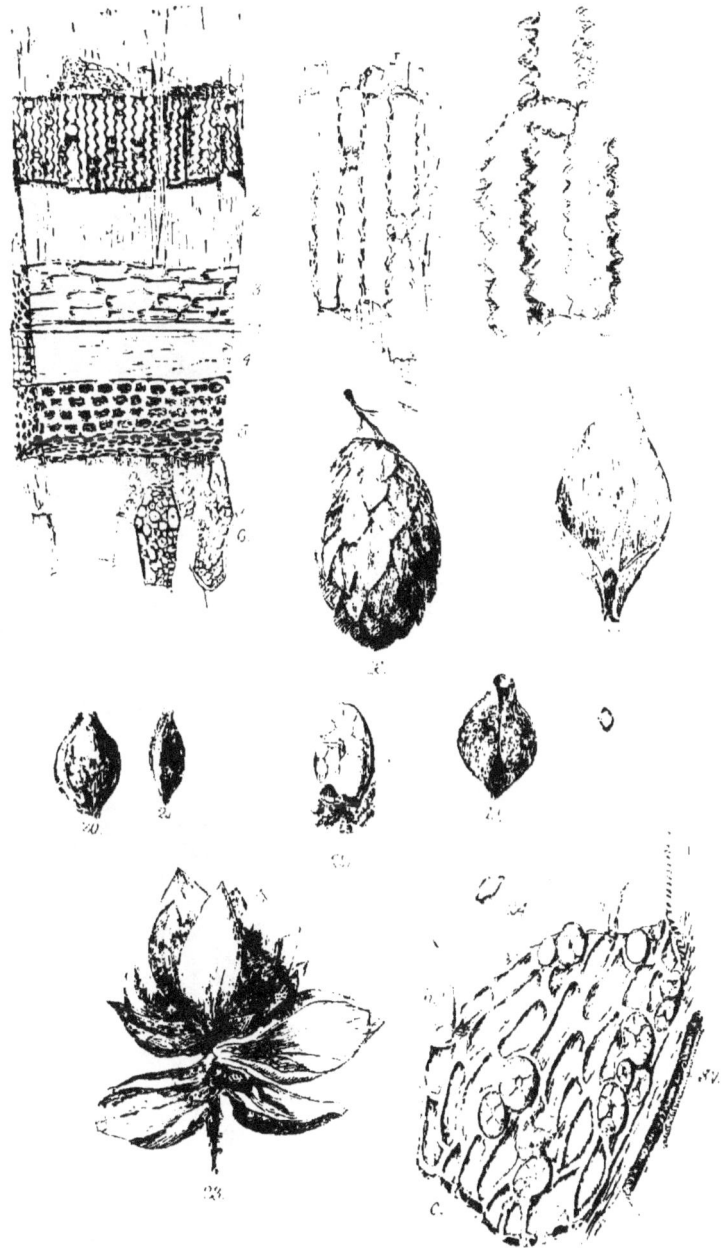

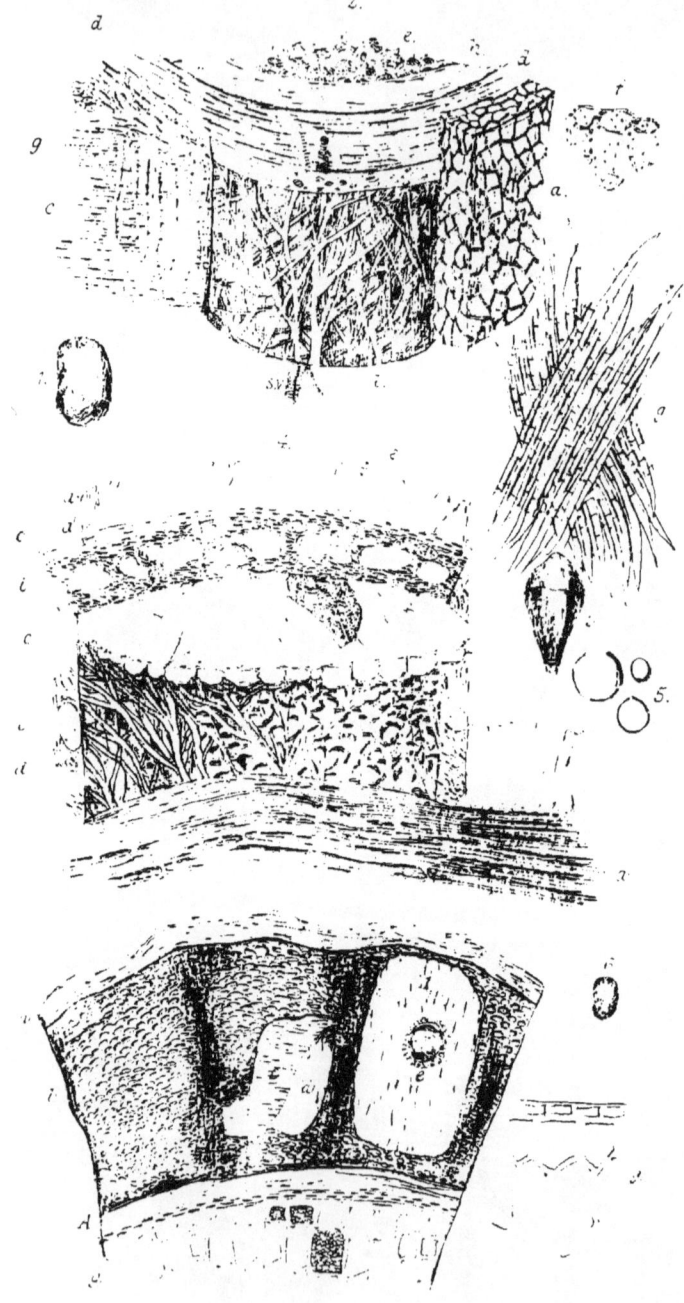

PLATE VII.

FIG.
1. A grain of Cocculus Indicus, n. s.
2. A diagram of the seed constructed from dissections; *a*, the outer skin, composed of irregularly-shaped cells full of dark brown colouring matter in three or four layers overlying; *b*, elongated branching fibrous cells, anastomosing amongst the elongated fibres (*c*) and the cylindrically formed wood cells at *g*: these form the hard or woody portion of the grain, in which are seen at intervals the spiral vessels (*s v*); *d*, layers of double-pointed fibres with thickened walls and lateral channels; *e*, albumen of the seed (cellular), containing much starch; *f*, cells of albumen separated to show their pores.
3. A grain of Paradise, magnified 8 diameters.
4. A diagram of the seed: *a*, the elongated wavy cells of the outer skin, overlying *b*, the woody tissue, amongst which are numerous oil receptacles, *o*: the branched fibres are seen anastomosing amongst these, *e*; *c*, the thin tough-walled cells of the albumen, containing abundance of minute starch granules.
5. Oil globules from the large *cysts* at *b*.
6. A grain of Datura Stramonium, magnified 2 diameters.
7. A horizontal diagram of the seed: *a*, long thin-walled cells of outer seed coat; *b*, layer of thick-walled coloured cells underlying it; *c*, a layer of long delicate cells underlying these, and overlying a layer of same form at a right angle to these; *e*, cyst containing dark brown colouring matter; *f*, a layer of long delicate cells with thin walls, and another of short cells with thick walls firmly attached to albumen (*g*), composed of very thick-walled cells laden with minute starch granules: *g*, cells of albumen very highly magnified.

PLATE VIII.

FIG.
25. A minute portion of a Hop leaf, viewed from its under side as an opaque object, and highly magnified to show the *lupulite* grains.
26. The seed of the hop, cut horizontally.
    a, 1. The outer seed coat, consisting of four or five rows of thick-walled cells with irregular outlines.
    2. Double-pointed ligneous cells, lined with *sclerogen* and with intercommunicating channels. *w* are the ends of elongated woody fibres, situated at right angles to these.
    b, 3. These thin layers of cells constitute a thin pellicle coloured bright green.
    4. A layer of oblong transparent cells.
    5. Another layer of thin-walled transparent cells; and at right angles to these, underlying them,—
    6. A series of coloured cells with thick walls overlying—
    c, 7. The albumen, containing much oil, here seen in globules forced out of the cells.
27. A small portion of the acorn-cup of the Valonia Oak, magnified, showing the woody cells lined with *sclerogen* (*w*) lying amongst the cellular tissue (*c*); *h h*, are the hairs on the exterior.
28. A portion of same, highly magnified. *a a*. are groups of large porous cells, which when dissected out are seen to have large intercommunicating channels: fig. 31.
29, 30. Branched and simple hairs, very highly magnified.

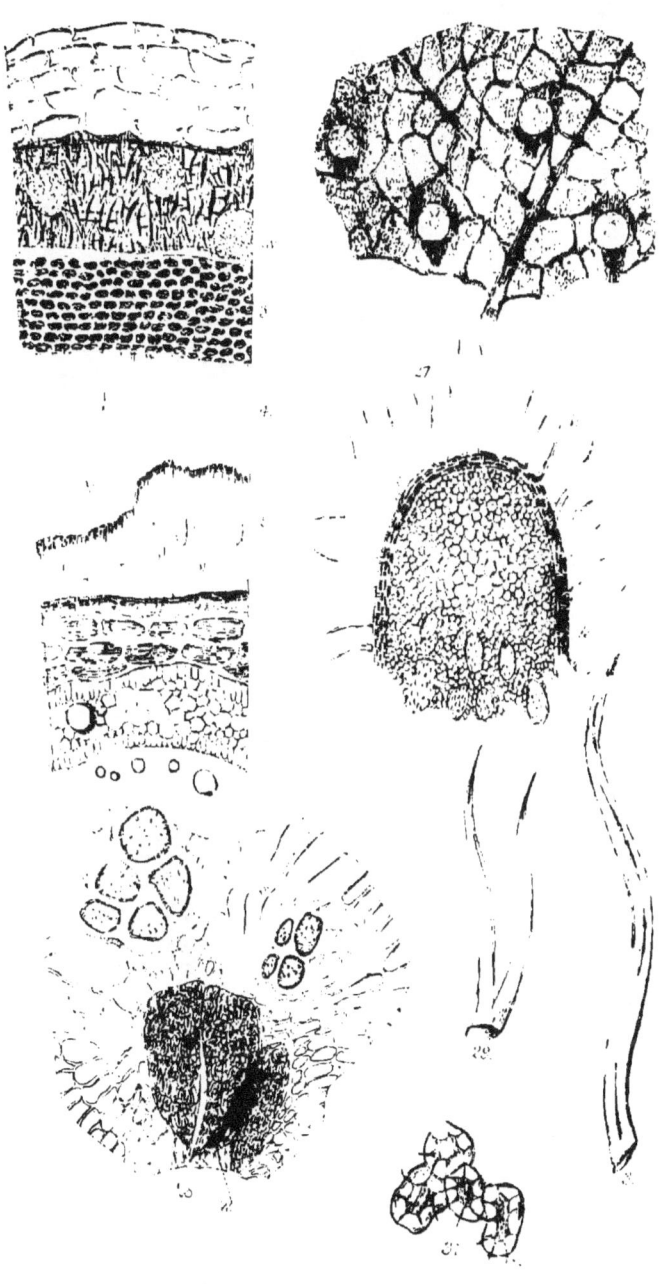

PLATE IX.

FIG.
1. A leaf of Virginian Tobacco attached to stem, $\frac{1}{4}$ n.s.
2. Portion of skin from under surface, greatly magnified, to show the two forms of hairs ($h\ h$) lying amongst the breathing pores, s.
3. Hairs separated, and highly magnified.
4. A transverse vertical section of portion of leaf-blade, with hairs and breathing pores on under surface.
5. A horizontal section of midrib of leaf, magnified.
6. A leaf of Burdock, $\frac{1}{8}$ n. s.
7. Hairs from under surface of leaf terminating in long delicate filaments, highly magnified.
8. Horizontal section of midrib of leaf with lobed outline, and bundles of woody fibre separated.
9. Leaf of Dock, $\frac{1}{8}$ n.s.; a, the stipule at base of stalk, detached.
10. Club-shaped, striated hairs, from skin of midrib and veins, greatly magnified.
11. Horizontal section of midrib, with lobed surface, and woody bundles separated.
12. A portion of skin of under side of leaf blade, greatly magnified, to show the position of the glands (g) amongst the breathing pores (s).

PLATE X.

FIG.
1. A leaf of Chicory, $\frac{1}{8}$ n. s.
2. A horizontal section from midrib of leaf, with thin woody bundles.
3. A portion of the skin removed from under side of leaf, greatly magnified to show the hairs on this part.
4. Leaf of Comfrey, $\frac{1}{8}$ n. s.
5. Horizontal section of midrib of leaf, showing the position and character of woody bundles.
6. A minute portion from the skin of the leaf on its under side, with *a*, large curved hairs with striated surfaces; *b b*, hairs formed like fish-hooks: very highly magnified.
7. Leaf of Jerusalem Artichoke, $\frac{1}{8}$ n. s., attached to stem.
8. Horizontal section of midrib of leaf, with woody bundles.
9. Epidermis from under side of leaf, greatly magnified, to show the peculiar form and texture of the hairs.

November, 1869.

16, BEDFORD STREET, COVENT GARDEN, LONDON.

MACMILLAN AND CO.'S
List of Publications.

ABBOTT.—*A Shakespearian Grammar.*
> An attempt to Illustrate some of the Differences between Elizabethan and Modern English. By E. A. ABBOTT, M.A. Head Master of the City of London School. *Second Edition.* Extra fcap. 8vo. 2s. 6d.

Æschyli Eumenides.
> The Greek Text with English Notes, and an Introduction. By BERNARD DRAKE, M.A. 8vo. 3s. 6d.

AIRY.—*Works by* G. B. AIRY, M.A. LL.D. D.C.L. *Astronomer Royal, &c.*

Treatise on the Algebraical and Numerical Theory of Errors of Observations and the Combination of Observations.
> Crown 8vo. 6s. 6d.

Popular Astronomy.
> A Series of Lectures delivered at Ipswich. *Sixth Edition.* 18mo. cloth, 4s. 6d. With Illustrations. Uniform with MACMILLAN'S SCHOOL CLASS BOOKS.

An Elementary Treatise on Partial Differential Equations.
> With Stereoscopic Cards of Diagrams. Crown 8vo. 5s. 6d.

On the Undulatory Theory of Optics.
> Designed for the use of Students in the University. Crown 8vo. 6s. 6d.

On Sound and Atmospheric Vibrations,
> With the Mathematical Elements of Music. Designed for the use of Students of the Universities. Crown 8vo. 9s.

Algebraical Exercises.
> Progressively arranged by Rev. C. A. JONES, M.A. and C. H. CHEYNE, M.A. Mathematical Masters in Westminster School. 18mo. 2s. 6d.

Alice's Adventures in Wonderland.
> By LEWIS CARROLL. With Forty-two Illustrations by TENNIEL. 18th Thousand. Crown 8vo. cloth. 6s.

A German Translation of the same.
> With TENNIEL'S Illustrations. Crown 8vo. gilt. 6s.

A French Translation of the same.
> With TENNIEL'S Illustrations. Crown 8vo. gilt. 6s.

A

15,000 11.69.

ALLINGHAM.—*Laurence Bloomfield in Ireland; or, The New Landlord.*
 Cheaper Issue, with New Preface. By WILLIAM ALLINGHAM. Fcap. 8vo. 4s 6d.

ANSTED.—*The Great Stone Book of Nature.*
 By DAVID THOMAS ANSTED, M.A. F.R.S. F.G.S. Fcap. 8vo. 5s.

ANSTIE.—*Stimulants and Narcotics, their Mutual Relations.*
 With Special Researches on the Action of Alcohol, Æther, and Chloroform on the Vital Organism. By FRANCIS E. ANSTIE, M.D. M.R.C.P. 8vo. 14s.

Neuralgia, and Diseases which resemble it.
 8vo.   [In the Press.

Aristotle on Fallacies; or, the Sophistici Elenchi.
 With a Translation and Notes by EDWARD POSTE, M.A. 8vo. 8s. 6d.

ARNOLD.—*Works by* MATTHEW ARNOLD.

The Complete Poetical Works.
  Vol. I.—*Narrative and Elegiac Poems.*
  Vol. II.—*Dramatic and Lyric Poems.*
 Extra fcap. 8vo. Price 6s. each.

New Poems. Second Edition.
 Extra fcap. 8vo. 6s. 6d.

A French Eton; or, Middle-Class Education and the State.
 Fcap. 8vo. 2s. 6d.

Essays in Criticism.
 New Edition, with Additions. Extra fcap. 8vo. 6s.

Schools and Universities on the Continent.
 8vo. 10s. 6d.

BAKER.—*Works by* SIR SAMUEL W. BAKER, M.A. F.R.G.S.

The Nile Tributaries of Abyssinia, and the Sword Hunters of the Hamran Arabs.
 With Portraits, Maps, and Illustrations. Third Edition. 8vo. 21s.

The Albert N'yanza Great Basin of the Nile, and Exploration of the Nile Sources. New and cheaper Edition.
 With Portraits, Maps, and Illustrations. Two Vols. crown 8vo. 16s.

Cast up by the Sea; or, The Adventures of Ned Grey.
 With Illustrations by HUARD. Second Edition. Crown 8vo. Cloth gilt. 7s. 6d.

BARNES.—*Poems of Rural Life in Common English.*
 By the Rev. W. BARNES, Author of "Poems of Rural Life in the Dorset Dialect." Fcap. 8vo. 6s.

BARWELL.—*Guide in the Sick Room.*
 By RICHARD BARWELL, F.R.C.S. Extra fcap. 8vo. 3s. 6d.

BATES AND LOCKYER.—*A Class-Book of Geography. Adapted to the recent programme of the Royal Geographical Society.*
 By H. W. BATES, Assistant Secretary to the Society, and J. N. LOCKYER, F.R.S. [In the Press.

BAXTER.—*Works by* R. DUDLEY BAXTER, M.A.
 National Income.
  With Coloured Diagram. 8vo. 3s. 6d.
 The Taxation of the United Kingdom. Its Amount, its Distribution, and Pressure.
  8vo. 4s. 6d.

BAYMA.—*Elements of Molecular Mechanics.*
 By JOSEPH BAYMA, S. J. 8vo. 10s. 6d.

BEASLEY.—*An Elementary Treatise on Plane Trigonometry.*
 With a Numerous Collection of Examples. By R. D. BEASLEY, M.A. Second Edition. Crown 8vo. 3s. 6d.

BELL.—*Romances and Minor Poems.*
 By HENRY GLASSFORD BELL. Fcap. 8vo. 6s.

BERNARD.—*The Progress of Doctrine in the New Testament.*
 In Eight Lectures preached before the University of Oxford. By THOMAS DEHANY BERNARD, M.A. Second Edition. 8vo. 8s. 6d.

BERNARD.—*Four Lectures on Subjects connected with Diplomacy.*
 By MOUNTAGUE BERNARD, M.A., Chichele Professor of International Law and Diplomacy, Oxford. 8vo. 9s.

BERNARD (ST.).—*The Life and Times of St. Bernard, Abbot of Clairvaux.*
 By J. C. MORISON, M.A. New Edition. Crown 8vo. 7s. 6d.

BESANT.—*Studies in Early French Poetry.*
 By WALTER BESANT, M.A. Crown 8vo. 8s. 6d.

BINNEY.—*Sermons preached in the King's Weigh House Chapel, 1829–1869.*
 By THOMAS BINNEY. New and Cheaper Edition, containing the "Farewell Sermon." Extra fcap. 8vo. 4s. 6d.

BIRKS.—*Works by* THOMAS RAWSON BIRKS, M.A.
  The Difficulties of Belief in connexion with the Creation and the Fall.
    Crown 8vo. 4s. 6d.
  On Matter and Ether ; or, the Secret Laws of Physical Change.
    Crown 8vo. 5s. 6d.

BLAKE.—*The Life of William Blake, the Artist.*
    By ALEXANDER GILCHRIST. With numerous Illustrations from Blake's Designs, and Fac-similes of his Studies of the "Book of Job." Two Vols. Medium 8vo. 32s.

Blanche Lisle, and other Poems.
    By CECIL HOME. Fcap. 8vo. 4s. 6d.

BOOLE.—*Works by the late* GEORGE BOOLE, F.R.S. *Professor of Mathematics in the Queen's University, Ireland, &c.*
  A Treatise on Differential Equations.
    New Edition. Edited by I. TODHUNTER, M.A. F.R.S. Crown 8vo. 14s.
  Treatise on Differential Equations.
    Supplementary Volume. Crown 8vo. 8s. 6d.
  A Treatise on the Calculus of Finite Differences.
    Crown 8vo. 10s. 6d.

BRADSHAW.—*An Attempt to ascertain the state of Chaucer's Works, as they were Left at his Death,*
    With some Notices of their Subsequent History. By HENRY BRADSHAW, of King's College, and the University Library, Cambridge.   [In the Press.

BRIGHT —*Speeches on Questions of Public Policy.*
    By the Right Honourable JOHN BRIGHT, M.P. Edited by PROFESSOR THOROLD ROGERS. *Second Edition.* 2 vols. 8vo. 25s With Portrait.
    Author's Popular Edition. Extra fcap. 8vo. 3s. 6d.

BRIMLEY.—*Essays by the late* GEORGE BRIMLEY, M.A.
    Edited by W. G. CLARK, M.A. With Portrait. *Cheaper Edition.* Fcap. 8vo. 3s. 6d.

BROOK SMITH.—*Arithmetic in Theory and Practice.*
    For Advanced Pupils. Part First. By J. BROOK SMITH, M.A. Crown 8vo. 3s. 6d.

BRYCE.—*The Holy Roman Empire.*
> By JAMES BRYCE, B.C.L. Fellow of Oriel College, Oxford. *A New Edition, revised and enlarged.* Crown 8vo. [In the Press.

BUCKNILL.—*The Mad Folk of Shakespeare.*
> Psychological Lectures by J. C. BUCKNILL, M.D. F.R.S. Second Edition. Crown 8vo. 6s. 6d.

BULLOCK.—*Works by* W. H. BULLOCK.
> *Polish Experiences during the Insurrection of* 1863-4.
> Crown 8vo. With Map. 8s. 6d.

> *Across Mexico in* 1864-5.
> With Coloured Map and Illustrations. Crown 8vo. 10s. 6d.

BURGON.—*A Treatise on the Pastoral Office.*
> Addressed chiefly to Candidates for Holy Orders, or to those who have recently undertaken the cure of souls. By the Rev. JOHN W. BURGON, M.A. 8vo. 12s.

BURNS.—*Globe Edition.*
> *The Poems, Letters, and Songs.*
> Being the Complete Works of Robert Burns. Edited, with Biographical Memoir, by ALEXANDER SMITH. Globe 8vo. 3s. 6d.

BUTLER (ARCHER).—*Works by the Rev.* WILLIAM ARCHER BUTLER, M.A. *late Professor of Moral Philosophy in the University of Dublin.*

> *Sermons, Doctrinal and Practical.*
> Edited, with a Memoir of the Author's Life, by THOMAS WOODWARD, M.A. Dean of Down. With Portrait. *Eighth and Cheaper Edition.* 8vo. 8s.

> *A Second Series of Sermons.*
> Edited by J. A. JEREMIE, D.D. Regius Professor of Divinity at Cambridge. *Fifth and Cheaper Edition.* 8vo. 7s.

> *History of Ancient Philosophy.*
> Edited by WM. H. THOMPSON, M.A. Master of Trinity College, Cambridge. Two Vols. 8vo. 1l. 5s.

> *Letters on Romanism, in reply to Dr. Newman's Essay on Development.*
> Edited by the Dean of Down. *Second Edition,* revised by Archdeacon HARDWICK. 8vo. 10s. 6d.

BUTLER (MONTAGU).—*Sermons preached in the Chapel of Harrow School.*
> By H. MONTAGU BUTLER, Head Master. Crown 8vo. 7s. 6d.
> ———— Second Series. Crown 8vo. 7s. 6d.

BUTLER (GEORGE). *Works by the Rev GEORGE BUTLER.*
Family Prayers
Crown 8vo. 5s.

Sermons preached in Cheltenham College Chapel.
Crown 8vo. 7s. 6d.

CAIRNES. *The Slave Power; its Character, Career, and Probable Designs.*
Being an Attempt to Explain the Real Issues Involved in the American Contest. By J. E. CAIRNES, M.A. Second Edition. 8vo. 10s. 6d.

CALDERWOOD. *Philosophy of the Infinite.*
A Treatise on Man's Knowledge of the Infinite Being, in answer to Sir W. Hamilton and Dr Mansel. By the Rev. HENRY CALDERWOOD, M.A. Professor of Moral Philosophy at Edinburgh. Second Edition. 8vo. 14s.

Cambridge Senate House Problems and Riders, with Solutions.

1848—1851 *Problems.*
By FERRERS and JACKSON. 8vo. 15s. 6d.

1848—1851 *Riders.*
By JAMESON. 8vo. 7s. 6d.

1854 *Problems and Riders.*
By WALTON and MACKENZIE, M.A. 8vo. 10s. 6d.

1857 *Problems and Riders.*
By CAMPION and WALTON. 8vo. 8s. 6d.

1860 *Problems and Riders.*
By WATSON and ROUTH. Crown 8vo. 7s. 6d.

1864 *Problems and Riders.*
By WALTON and WILKINSON. 8vo. 10s. 6d.

Cambridge Lent Sermons.
Sermons preached during Lent, 1864, in Great St. Mary's Church, Cambridge. By the Bishop of OXFORD, Rev. H. P. LIDDON, T. L. CLAUGHTON, J. R. WOODFORD, Dr GOULBURN, J. W. BURGON, T. T. CARTER, Dr PUSEY, DEAN HOOK, W. J. BUTLER, DEAN GOODWIN. Crown 8vo. 7s. 6d.

Cambridge Course of Elementary Natural Philosophy, for the Degree of B.A.
Originally compiled by J. C. SNOWBALL, M.A., late Fellow of St John's College. Fifth Edition, revised and enlarged, and adapted for the Middle Class Examinations by THOMAS LUND, B.D. Crown 8vo. 5s.

Cambridge and Dublin Mathematical Journal
 The Complete Work, in Nine Vols. 8vo. Cloth 7l. 6s. Only a few copies remain on hand.

Cambridge Union Society's Inaugural Proceedings
 Fcap. 8vo. 3s.

Cambridge Characteristics in the Seventeenth Century.
 By JAMES BASS MULLINGER, B.A. Crown 8vo. 4s. 6d.

CAMPBELL. Works by JOHN M'LEOD CAMPBELL.
 Thoughts on Revelation, with Special Reference to the Present Time.
  Crown 8vo. 5s.
 The Nature of the Atonement, and its Relation to Remission of Sins and Eternal Life.
  Third Edition. With an Introduction and Notes. 8vo. 10s. 6d.
 Christ the Bread of Life.
  An attempt to give a profitable direction to the present occupation of thought with Romanism. Second Edition. Greatly enlarged. Crown 8vo. 4s. 6d.

CANDLER. *Help to Arithmetic, designed for the Use of Schools.*
 By H. CANDLER, M.A. Mathematical Master at Uppingham. Fcap. 8vo. 2s. 6d.

CARTER. *King's College Chapel; Notes on its History and present condition.*
 By T. J. P. CARTER, M.A. Fellow of King's College, Cambridge. With Photographs. 8vo. 6s.

Catullus.
 Edited by R. ELLIS. 18mo. 3s. 6d.

CHALLIS. *Creation in Plan and in Progress:*
 Being an Essay on the First Chapter of Genesis. By the Rev. JAMES CHALLIS, M.A. F.R.S. F.R.A.S. Crown 8vo. 3s. 6d.

CHATTERTON. *Leonore; a Tale.*
 By GEORGIANA LADY CHATTERTON. A New Edition. Beautifully printed on thick toned paper. Crown 8vo. with Frontispiece and Vignette Title engraved by JEENS. 7s. 6d.

CHEYNE. Works by C. H. H. CHEYNE, B.A.
 An Elementary Treatise on the Planetary Theory.
  With a Collection of Problems. Crown 8vo. 6s. 6d.
 The Earth's Motion of Rotation (including the Theory of Precession and Nutation).
  Crown 8vo. 3s. 6d.

CHEYNE.—*Notes and Criticisms on the Hebrew Text of Isaiah.*
By the Rev. T. K. CHEYNE, M.A. Fellow of Balliol College,
Oxford. 8vo. 2s. 6d.

*Choice Notes on the Four Gospels, drawn from Old and New
Sources.*
Crown 8vo. 4s. 6d. each Vol. (St. Matthew and St. Mark in
One Vol. price 9s.)

CHRISTIE (J. R.).—*Elementary Test Questions in Pure and
Mixed Mathematics.*
Crown 8vo. 8s. 6d.

Church Congress (Authorized Report of) held at Wolverhampton in October, 1867.
8vo. 3s. 6d.

CHURCH.—*Sermons preached before the University of Oxford.*
By R. W. CHURCH, M.A. late Fellow of Oriel College, Rector of
Whatley. Crown 8vo. 4s. 6d. *Second Edition.*

CICERO.—*The Second Philippic Oration.*
With an Introduction and Notes, translated from KARL HALM.
Edited, with Corrections and Additions, by JOHN E. B. MAYOR,
M.A. *Third Edition.* Fcap. 8vo. 5s.

CLARK.—*Four Sermons preached in the Chapel of Trinity
College, Cambridge.*
By W. G. CLARK, M.A. Fcap. 8vo. 2s. 6d.

AY.—*The Prison Chaplain.*
A Memoir of the Rev. JOHN CLAY, B.D. late Chaplain of the
Preston Gaol. With Selections from his Reports and Correspondence, and a Sketch of Prison Discipline in England. By
his Son, the Rev. W. L. CLAY, M.A. 8vo. 15s.

The Power of the Keys.
Sermons preached in Coventry. By the Rev. W. L. CLAY, M.A.
Fcap. 8vo. 3s. 6d.

Clemency Franklyn.
By the author of "Janet's Home." Crown 8vo. 6s.

Clergyman's Self-Examination concerning the Apostles' Creed.
Extra fcap 8vo. 1s. 6d.

CLOUGH.—*The Poems of Arthur Hugh Clough,*
sometime Fellow of Oriel College, Oxford. With a Memoir by
F. T. PALGRAVE. *Second Edition.* Fcap. 8vo. 6s.

CLOUGH.—*The Poems and Prose Remains of Arthur Hugh Clough.*
    Edited by his Wife. With a Selection from his Letters, and a Memoir. 2 vols. Crown 8vo. 21s.

COLENSO.—*Works by the Right Rev.* J. W. COLENSO, D.D. *Bishop of Natal.*

The Colony of Natal.
    A Journal of Visitation. With a Map and Illustrations. Fcap. 8vo. 5s.

Village Sermons.
    Second Edition. Fcap. 8vo. 2s. 6d.

Companion to the Holy Communion,
    Containing the Service and Select Readings from the writings of Professor MAURICE. Common paper, 1s.

Connells of Castle Connell.
    By JANET GORDON. Two Vols. Crown 8vo. 21s.

COOPER.—*Athenae Cantabrigienses.*
    By CHARLES HENRY COOPER, F.S.A. and THOMPSON COOPER, F.S.A. Vol. I. 8vo. 1500—85, 18s. Vol. II. 1586—1609, 18s.

COPE.—*An Introduction to Aristotle's Rhetoric.*
    With Analysis, Notes, and Appendices. By E. M. COPE, Senior Fellow and Tutor of Trinity College, Cambridge. 8vo. 14s.

COTTON.—*Works by the late* GEORGE EDWARD LYNCH COTTON, D.D. *Bishop of Calcutta.*

Sermons and Addresses delivered in Marlborough College during Six Years.
    Crown 8vo. 10s. 6d.

Sermons, chiefly connected with Public Events of 1854.
    Fcap. 8vo. 3s.

Sermons preached to English Congregations in India.
    Crown 8vo. 7s. 6d.

Expository Sermons on the Epistles for the Sundays of the Christian Year.
    Two Vols. Crown 8vo. 15s.

COX.—*Recollections of Oxford.*
    By G. V. COX, M.A. late Esquire Bedel and Coroner in the University of Oxford. Crown 8vo. 10s. 6d.

CURE.—*The Seven Words of Christ on the Cross.*
    Sermons preached at St. George's, Bloomsbury. By the Rev. E. CAPEL CURE, M.A. Fcap. 8vo. 3s. 6d.

DALTON.—*Arithmetical Examples progressively arranged; together with Miscellaneous Exercises and Examination Papers.*
    By the Rev. T. DALTON, M.A. Assistant Master at Eton College. 18mo. 2s 6d.

DANTE.—*Dante's Comedy, The Hell.*
    Translated by W. M. ROSSETTI. Fcap. 8vo. cloth. 5s.

DAVIES.—*Works by the Rev. J. LLEWELYN DAVIES, M.A. Rector of Christ Church, St. Marylebone, &c.*

Sermons on the Manifestation of the Son of God.
    With a Preface addressed to Laymen on the present position of the Clergy of the Church of England; and an Appendix, on the Testimony of Scripture and the Church as to the Possibility of Pardon in the Future State. Fcap. 8vo. 6s. 6d.

The Work of Christ; or, the World Reconciled to God.
    With a Preface on the Atonement Controversy. Fcap. 8vo. 6s.

Baptism, Confirmation, and the Lord's Supper.
    As interpreted by their outward signs. Three Expository Addresses for Parochial Use. Fcap. 8vo. Limp cloth. 1s. 6d.

Morality according to the Sacrament of the Lord's Supper.
    Crown 8vo. 3s. 6d.

The Epistles of St. Paul to the Ephesians, the Colossians, and Philemon.
    With Introductions and Notes, and an Essay on the Traces of Foreign Elements in the Theology of these Epistles. 8vo. 7s. 6d.

The Gospel and Modern Life.
    Sermons on some of the Difficulties of the Present Day. With a Preface on a Recent Phase of Deism. Extra fcap. 8vo. 6s.

DAWSON.—*Acadian Geology, the Geological Structure, Organic Remains, and Mineral Resources of Nova Scotia, New Brunswick, and Prince Edward Island.*
    By J. W. DAWSON, LL.D. F.R.S. F.G.S. *Second Edition*, revised and enlarged, with Geological Maps and Illustrations. 8vo. 18s.

DAY.—*Properties of Conic Sections proved Geometrically.*
 By the Rev. H. G. DAY, M.A. Head-Master of Sedbergh Grammar School. Crown 8vo. 3s. 6d.

Days of Old ; Stories from Old English History.
 By the Author of "Ruth and her Friends." New Edition, 18mo. cloth, gilt leaves. 3s. 6d.

DELAMOTTE.—*A Beginner's Drawing Book.*
 By PHILIP H. DELAMOTTE, F.S.A. Professor of Drawing in King's College and School, London. Progressively arranged. With upwards of Fifty Plates. Stiff Covers, crown 8vo. 2s. 6d.

Demosthenes, De Corona.
 The Greek Text with English Notes. By B. DRAKE, M.A. Third Edition, to which is prefixed ÆSCHINES AGAINST CTESIPHON, with English Notes. Fcap 8vo. 5s.

DE TEISSIER.— *Works by* G. F. DE TEISSIER, B.D.
Village Sermons.
 Crown 8vo. 9s.
Second Series.
 Crown 8vo. 8s. 6d.
The House of Prayer ; or, a Practical Exposition of the Order for Morning and Evening Prayer in the Church of England.
 18mo. extra cloth. 4s. 6d.

DE VERE.—*The Infant Bridal, and other Poems.*
 By AUBREY DE VERE. Fcap. 8vo. 7s. 6d.

DILKE.—*Greater Britain.*
 A Record of Travel in English-speaking Countries during 1866-7. (America, Australia, India.) By Sir CHARLES WENTWORTH DILKE, M.P. *Fourth and Cheaper Edition.* Crown 8vo. 6s.

DODGSON.—*Elementary Treatise on Determinants.*
 By C. L. DODGSON, M.A. 4to. 10s. 6d.

DONALDSON.—*A Critical History of Christian Literature and Doctrine, from the Death of the Apostles to the Nicene Council.*
 By JAMES DONALDSON, LL.D. Three Vols. 8vo. cloth. 31s.

DOYLE.— *Works by Sir* FRANCIS HASTINGS DOYLE, *Professor of Poetry in the University of Oxford.*
The Return of the Guards, and other Poems.
 Fcap. 8vo. 7s.
Lectures on Poetry.
 Delivered before the University of Oxford in 1868. Crown 8vo. 3s. 6d.

DREW.—*Works by* W. H. DREW, M.A.

A Geometrical Treatise on Conic Sections.
Fourth Edition. Crown 8vo. 4s. 6d.

Solutions to Problems contained in Drew's Treatise on Conic Sections.
Crown 8vo. 4s. 6d.

DÜRER (ALBRECHT).—*The History of the Life of Albrecht Dürer of Nürnberg, with a Translation of his Letters and Journal, and some Account of his Works.*
By Mrs. CHARLES HEATON. With Thirty Photographic and Antotype Illustrations. Royal 8vo. 31s. 6d.

Early Egyptian History for the Young.
With Descriptions of the Tombs and Monuments. *New Edition*, with Frontispiece. Fcap. 8vo. 5s.

EASTWOOD.—*The Bible Word Book.*
A Glossary of Old English Bible Words. By J. EASTWOOD, M.A. of St. John's College, and W. ALDIS WRIGHT, M.A. Trinity College, Cambridge. 18mo. 5s. 6d. Uniform with Macmillan's School Class Books.

Ecce Homo.
A Survey of the Life and Work of Jesus Christ. 23d Thousand. Crown 8vo. 6s.

Echoes of Many Voices from Many Lands.
By A. F. 18mo. cloth, extra gilt. 3s. 6d.

EDGAR.—*Note Book on Practical Solid Geometry, containing Problems with Help for Solution.*
By J. H. EDGAR, M.A. Lecturer on Mechanical Drawing in the Royal School of Mines, London. 4to. 2s.

ELAM.—*A Physician's Problems.*
By CHARLES ELAM, M.D. M.R.C.P. Contents : Natural Heritage—On Degenerations in Man—On Moral and Criminal Epidemics—Body v. Mind—Illusions and Hallucinations—On Somnambulism—Reverie and Abstraction. Crown 8vo. 9s.

ELLICE.—*English Idylls.*
By JANE ELLICE. Fcap. 8vo. cloth. 6s.

ELLIOTT.—*Life of Henry Venn Elliott, of Brighton.*
By JOSIAH BATEMAN, M.A. Author of "Life of Daniel Wilson, Bishop of Calcutta," &c. With Portrait, engraved by JEENS. Crown 8vo. 8s. 6d.

ERLE.—*The Law relating to Trade Unions.*
> By Sir WILLIAM ERLE, formerly Chief Justice in the Common Pleas. Crown 8vo. 3s. 6d.

Essays on Church Policy.
> Edited by the Rev. W. L. CLAY, M.A. Incumbent of Rainhill, Lancashire. 8vo. 9s.

Essays on a Liberal Education.
> By Various Writers. Edited by the Rev. F. W. FARRAR, M.A. F.R.S. &c. Second Edition. 8vo. 10s. 6d.

EVANS.—*Brother Fabian's Manuscript, and other Poems.*
> By SEBASTIAN EVANS. Fcap. 8vo. cloth. 6s.

FARRAR.—*The Fall of Man, and other Sermons.*
> By the Rev. F. W. FARRAR, M.A. late Fellow of Trinity College, Cambridge. Fcap. 8vo. 6s.

FAWCETT.—*Works by* HENRY FAWCETT, M.P.

The Economic Position of the British Labourer.
> Extra fcap. 8vo. 5s.

Manual of Political Economy.
> Second Edition. Crown 8vo. 12s.

Fellowship: Letters addressed to my Sister Mourners.
> Fcap. 8vo. cloth gilt. 3s. 6d.

FERRERS.—*A Treatise on Trilinear Co-ordinates, the Method of Reciprocal Polars, and the Theory of Projections.*
> By the Rev. N. M. FERRERS, M.A. Second Edition. Crown 8vo. 6s. 6d.

FLETCHER.—*Thoughts from a Girl's Life.*
> By LUCY FLETCHER. Second Edition. Fcap. 8vo. 4s. 6d.

FORBES.—*Life of Edward Forbes, F.R.S.*
> By GEORGE WILSON, M.D. F.R.S.E., and ARCHIBALD GEIKIE, F.R.S. 8vo. with Portrait. 14s.

FORBES.—*The Voice of God in the Psalms.*
> By GRANVILLE FORBES, Rector of Broughton. Crown 8vo. 6s. 6d.

FOX.—*On the Diagnosis and Treatment of the Varieties of Dyspepsia, considered in Relation to the Pathological Origin of the different Forms of Indigestion.*
> By WILSON FOX, M.D. Lond. F.R.C.P. Holme Professor of Clinical Medicine at University College, London, and Physician to University College Hospital. Second Edition Demy 8vo. 7s. 6d.

FOX.—*On the Artificial Production of Tubercle in the Lower Animals.*
    4to. 5s. 6d.

FREELAND.—*The Fountain of Youth.*
    Translated from the Danish of Frederick Paludan Müller. By HUMPHREY WILLIAM FREELAND, late M.P. for Chichester. With Illustrations designed by Walter Allen. Crown 8vo. 6s.

FREEMAN.—*History of Federal Government from the Foundation of the Achaian League to the Disruption of the United States.*
    By EDWARD A. FREEMAN, M.A. Vol. I. General Introduction. —History of the Greek Federations. 8vo. 21s.

Old English History for Children.
    With Five Coloured Maps. Extra fcap. 8vo. 6s.

FRENCH.—*Shakspeareana Genealogica.*
    PART I.—Identification of the Dramatis Personæ in the Historical Plays, from King John to King Henry VIII.: Notes on Characters in Macbeth and Hamlet: Persons and Places belonging to Warwickshire alluded to. PART II.—The Shakspeare and Arden Families and their Connections, with Tables of Descent. By GEORGE RUSSELL FRENCH. 8vo. 15s.

FROST.—*The First Three Sections of Newton's Principia.*
    With Notes and Problems in Illustration of the Subject By PERCIVAL FROST, M.A. *Second Edition.* 8vo. 10s. 6d.

FROST AND WOLSTENHOLME.—*A Treatise on Solid Geometry.*
    By the Rev. PERCIVAL FROST, M.A. and the Rev. J. WOLSTENHOLME, M.A. 8vo. 18s.

The Sicilian Expedition.
    Being Books VI. and VII. of Thucydides, with Notes. By the Rev. P. FROST, M.A. *New Edition.* Fcap. 8vo. 5s.

FURNIVALL.—*Le Morte Arthur.*
    Edited from the Harleian M.S. 2252, in the British Museum. By F. J. FURNIVALL, M.A. With Essay by the late HERBERT COLERIDGE. Fcap. 8vo. 7s. 6d.

GALTON.—*Works by* FRANCIS GALTON, F.R.S.

Meteorographica, or Methods of Mapping the Weather.
    Illustrated by upwards of 600 Printed Lithographed Diagrams. By FRANCIS GALTON, F.R.S. 4to. 9s.

Hereditary Genius, its Laws and Consequences.
    With numerous illustrative Examples. [In the Press.

GARNETT.—*Idylls and Epigrams.*
>Chiefly from the Greek Anthology. By RICHARD GARNETT. Fcap. 8vo. 2s. 6d.

GEIKIE.—*Works by* ARCHIBALD GEIKIE, F.R.S. *Director of the Geological Survey of Scotland.*

Story of a Boulder; or, Gleanings by a Field Geologist.
>Illustrated with Woodcuts. Crown 8vo. 5s.

Scenery of Scotland, viewed in connexion with its Physical Geology.
>With Illustrations and a New Geological Map. Crown 8vo. 10s. 6d.

Elementary Lessons in Physical Geology. [In the Press.

GIFFORD.—*The Glory of God in Man.*
>By E. H. GIFFORD, D.D. Fcap. 8vo. 3s. 6d.

GLADSTONE.—*Juventus Mundi: Gods and Men of the Greek Heroic Age.*
>With Map of the outer Geography of the Odyssey. By the Right Hon. W. E. GLADSTONE, M.P. Crown 8vo. 10s. 6d.

Globe Editions :

The Complete Works of William Shakespeare.
>Edited by W. G. CLARK and W. ALDIS WRIGHT. Ninety-first Thousand. Globe 8vo. 3s. 6d.

Morte DArthur.
>SIR THOMAS MALORY'S Book of KING ARTHUR and of his noble KNIGHTS of the ROUND TABLE. The Edition of Caxton, revised for Modern use. With an Introduction by SIR EDWARD STRACHEY, Bart. Globe 8vo. 3s. 6d. *Second Edition.*

The Poetical Works of Sir Walter Scott.
>With Biographical and Critical Essay by F. T. PALGRAVE.

The Poetical Works and Letters of Robert Burns.
>Edited, with Life and Glossarial Index, by ALEXANDER SMITH. Globe 8vo. 3s. 6d.

The Adventures of Robinson Crusoe.
>Edited, from the Original Editions, with Introduction, by HENRY KINGSLEY. Globe 8vo. 3s. 6d.

Goldsmith's Miscellaneous Works.
>With Biographical Essay by PROF. MASSON. Globe 8vo. 3s. 6d.

Globe Editions:

Alexander Pope's Poetical Works.
Edited, with Memoir and Notes, by PROFESSOR WARD. Globe 8vo. 3s. 6d.

Spenser's Complete Works.
Edited by R. MORRIS. With Memoir by J. W. HALES, M.A. Globe 8vo. 3s. 6d.

Other Standard Works are in the Press.

Globe Atlas of Europe.
Uniform in Size with MACMILLAN'S GLOBE SERIES. Containing Forty-Eight Coloured Maps on the same scale, Plans of London and Paris, and a Copious Index. Strongly bound in half morocco, with flexible back, 9s.

GODFRAY.—*An Elementary Treatise on the Lunar Theory.*
With a brief Sketch of the Problem up to the time of Newton. By HUGH GODFRAY, M.A. *Second Edition revised.* Crown 8vo. 5s. 6d.

A Treatise on Astronomy, for the Use of Colleges and Schools.
By HUGH GODFRAY, M.A. 8vo. 12s. 6d.

Golden Treasury Series:
Uniformly printed in 18mo. with Vignette Titles by Sir NOEL PATON, T. WOOLNER, W. HOLMAN HUNT, J. E. MILLAIS, ARTHUR HUGHES, &c. Engraved on Steel by JEENS. Bound in extra cloth, 4s. 6d.

The Golden Treasury of the Best Songs and Lyrical Poems in the English Language.
Selected and arranged, with Notes, by FRANCIS TURNER PALGRAVE.

The Children's Garland from the Best Poets.
Selected and arranged by COVENTRY PATMORE.

The Book of Praise.
From the Best English Hymn Writers. Selected and arranged by Sir ROUNDELL PALMER. *A New and Enlarged Edition.*

The Fairy Book: the Best Popular Fairy Stories.
Selected and rendered anew by the Author of "John Halifax, Gentleman."

The Ballad Book.
A Selection of the choicest British Ballads. Edited by WILLIAM ALLINGHAM.

The Jest Book.
The choicest Anecdotes and Sayings. Selected and arranged by MARK LEMON.

Golden Treasury Series—continued.

Bacon's Essays and Colours of Good and Evil.
With Notes and Glossarial Index, by W. ALDIS WRIGHT, M.A.
⁎ Large paper copies, crown 8vo. 7s. 6d.; or bound in half morocco, 10s. 6d.

The Pilgrim's Progress
From this World to that which is to Come. By JOHN BUNYAN.
⁎ Large paper copies, crown 8vo. cloth, 7s. 6d.; or bound in half morocco, 10s. 6d.

The Sunday Book of Poetry for the Young.
Selected and arranged by C. F. ALEXANDER.

A Book of Golden Deeds of all Times and all Countries.
Gathered and Narrated anew by the Author of "The Heir of Redclyffe."

The Poetical Works of Robert Burns.
Edited, with Biographical Memoir, by ALEXANDER SMITH. Two Vols.

The Adventures of Robinson Crusoe.
Edited from the Original Editions by J. W. CLARK, M.A.

The Republic of Plato.
Translated into English with Notes by J. LL. DAVIES, M.A. and D. J. VAUGHAN, M.A.

The Song Book.
Words and Tunes from the best Poets and Musicians, selected and arranged by JOHN HULLAH.

La Lyre Française.
Selected and arranged, with Notes, by GUSTAVE MASSON.

Tom Brown's School Days.
By an OLD BOY.

A Book of Worthies.
Gathered from the old Histories and written anew by the Author of "The Heir of Redclyffe."

GOLDSMITH.—*Globe Edition.*

The Miscellaneous Works of Oliver Goldsmith.
With Biographical Essay by PROFESSOR MASSON. Globe 8vo. 3s. 6d.

GREEN.—*Spiritual Philosophy.*
Founded on the Teaching of the late SAMUEL TAYLOR COLERIDGE. By the late JOSEPH HENRY GREEN, F.R.S. D.C.L. Edited, with a Memoir of the Author's Life, by JOHN SIMON F.R.S. Two Vols. 8vo. cloth. 25s.

Guesses at Truth.
> By Two Brothers. With Vignette Title and Frontispiece. *New Edition.* Fcap. 8vo. 6s.

Guizot, M.—*Memoir of M. de Barante.*
> Translated by the Author of "John Halifax, Gentleman." Crown 8vo. 6s. 6d.

Guide to the Unprotected
> In Every Day Matters relating to Property and Income. By a Banker's Daughter. *Third Edition.* Extra fcap. 8vo. 3s. 6d.

Hales and Twentyman.—*A Selection of Longer English Poems for Use in Schools.*
> With Explanatory Notes, &c. By J. W. Hales and J. Twentyman. Extra fcap. 8vo. [In the Press.

Hamerton.—*A Painter's Camp in the Highlands.*
> By P. G. Hamerton. *New and Cheaper Edition*, one vol. Extra fcap. 8vo. 6s.

Etching and Etchers.
> A Treatise Critical and Practical. By P. G. Hamerton. With Original Plates by Rembrandt, Callot, Dujardin, Paul Potter, &c. Royal 8vo. Half morocco. 31s. 6d.

Hamilton.—*On Truth and Error.*
> Thoughts on the Principles of Truth, and the Causes and Effect of Error. By John Hamilton. Crown 8vo. 5s.

Arthur's Seat; or, The Church of the Banned.
> By John Hamilton. Crown 8vo. 6s.

Hardwick.—*Works by the Ven.* Archdeacon Hardwick.
Christ and other Masters.
> A Historical Inquiry into some of the Chief Parallelisms and Contrasts between Christianity and the Religious Systems of the Ancient World. *New Edition*, revised, and a Prefatory Memoir by the Rev. Francis Procter, M.A. Two vols. crown 8vo. 15s.

A History of the Christian Church.
> Middle Age. From Gregory the Great to the Excommunication of Luther. Edited by Francis Procter, M.A. With Four Maps constructed for this work by A. Keith Johnston. *Second Edition.* Crown 8vo. 10s. 6d.

A History of the Christian Church during the Reformation.
> Revised by Francis Procter, M.A. *Second Edition.* Crown 8vo. 10s. 6d.

Twenty Sermons for Town Congregations.
> Crown 8vo. 6s. 6d.

HARLEY.—*The Old Vegetable Neurotics, Hemlock, Opium, Belladonna, and Henbane:*
> Their Physiological Action and Therapeutical Use, Alone and in Combination. Being the Gulstonian Lectures of 1868 extended, and including a complete Examination of the Active Constituents of Opium. By JOHN HARLEY, M.D. Lond. 8vo. 12s.

HELPS.—*Realmah.*
> By ARTHUR HELPS. Two vols. crown 8vo. 16s.

HEMMING.—*An Elementary Treatise on the Differential and Integral Calculus.*
> By G. W. HEMMING, M.A. *Second Edition.* 8vo. 9s.

HERSCHEL.—*The Iliad of Homer.*
> Translated into English Hexameters. By Sir JOHN HERSCHEL, Bart. 8vo. 18s.

HERVEY.—*The Genealogies of our Lord and Saviour Jesus Christ,*
> As contained in the Gospels of St. Matthew and St. Luke, reconciled with each other, and shown to be in harmony with the true Chronology of the Times. By Lord ARTHUR HERVEY, M.A. 8vo. 10s. 6d.

HERVEY (ROSAMOND). *Works by* ROSAMOND HERVEY.

The Aarbergs.
> Two vols. crown 8vo. cloth. 21s.

Duke Ernest,
> A Tragedy; and other Poems. Fcap. 8vo. 6s.

Hiatus: the Void in Modern Education.
> Its Cause and Antidote. By OUTIS. 8vo. 8s. 6d.

HIGGINSON.—*Malbone:*
> An Old Port Romance. By T. W. HIGGINSON. Fcap. 8vo. 2s. 6d.

HILL (FLORENCE).—*Children of the State. The Training of Juvenile Paupers.*
> Extra fcap. 8vo. cloth. 5s.

Historical Selections.
> A Series of Readings from the best Authorities on English and European History. Selected and Arranged by E. M. SEWELL and C. M. YONGE. Extra fcap. 8vo. 6s.

HISTORICUS.—*Letters on some Questions of International Law.*
> Reprinted from the *Times*, with considerable Additions. 8vo. 7s. 6d. Also, ADDITIONAL LETTERS. 8vo. 2s. 6d.

HODGSON.—*Mythology for Latin Versification.*
    A Brief Sketch of the Fables of the Ancients, prepared to be rendered into Latin Verse for Schools. By F. HODGSON, B.D. late Provost of Eton. *New Edition*, revised by F. C. HODGSON, M.A. 18mo. 3s.

HOLE.—*Works by* CHARLES HOLE, *M.A. Trinity College, Cambridge.*
    A Brief Biographical Dictionary.
        Compiled and arranged by CHARLES HOLE, M.A. Trinity College, Cambridge. *Second Edition.* 18mo. 4s. 6d.
    Genealogical Stemma of the Kings of England and France.
        In One Sheet. 1s.

HORNER.—*The Tuscan Poet Guiseppe Giusti and his Times.*
    By SUSAN HORNER. Crown 8vo. 7s. 6d.

HOWARD.—*The Pentateuch;*
    Or, the Five Books of Moses. Translated into English from the Version of the LXX. With Notes on its Omissions and Insertions, and also on the Passages in which it differs from the Authorized Version. By the Hon. HENRY HOWARD, D.D. Crown 8vo. GENESIS, One Volume, 8s. 6d.; EXODUS AND LEVITICUS, One Volume, 10s. 6d.; NUMBERS AND DEUTERONOMY, One Volume, 10s. 6d.

HOZIER.—*The Seven Weeks' War;*
    Its Antecedents and its Incidents. By H. M. HOZIER. With Maps and Plans. Two Vols. 8vo. 28s.
    The British Expedition in Abyssinia.
        Compiled from Official and Authentic Documents. By CAPTAIN H. M. HOZIER, late Assistant Military Secretary to Lord Napier of Magdala. 8vo. 9s.

HUMPHRY.—*The Human Skeleton (including the Joints).*
    By G. M. HUMPHRY, M.D., F.R.S. With Two Hundred and Sixty Illustrations drawn from Nature. Medium 8vo. 1l. 8s.

HUXLEY.—*Lessons in Elementary Physiology.*
    With numerous Illustrations. By T. H. HUXLEY, F.R.S. Professor of Natural History in the Royal School of Mines. Uniform with Macmillan's School Class Books. *Third Edition.* 18mo. 4s. 6d.

Huxley's Physiology, Questions on, for Schools.
    By T. ALCOCK, M.D. 18mo. 1s. 6d.

Hymni Ecclesiæ.
    Fcap. 8vo. 7s. 6d.

IRVING.—*Annals of our Time.*
: A Diurnal of Events, Social and Political, which have happened in or had relation to the Kingdom of Great Britain from the Accession of Queen Victoria to the Opening of the present Parliament. By JOSEPH IRVING. 8vo. half-bound. 18s.

JAMESON.—*Works by the Rev.* F. J. JAMESON, M.A.

Life's Work, in Preparation and in Retrospect.
: Sermons preached before the University of Cambridge. Fcap. 8vo. 1s. 6d.

Brotherly Counsels to Students.
: Sermons preached in the Chapel of St. Catharine's College, Cambridge. Fcap. 8vo. 1s. 6d.

JEVONS.—*The Coal Question.*
: By W. STANLEY JEVONS, M.A. Professor of Logic, Queen's College, Manchester. *Second Edition, revised.* 8vo. 10s. 6d.

The Substitution of Similars the True Principle of Reasoning;
: Derived from a Modification of Aristotle's Dictum. Fcap. 8vo. 2s. 6d.

JEX-BLAKE.—*A Visit to some American Schools and Colleges.*
: By SOPHIA JEX-BLAKE. Crown 8vo. 6s.

JOHNSON.—*How Crops Grow.*
: A Treatise on the Chemical Composition, Structure, and Life of the Plant, for Agricultural Students. With numerous Illustrations and Tables of Analyses. By S. W. JOHNSON, M.A. Revised, with numerous additions, and adapted for English use, by A. H. CHURCH, M.A. and W. T. DYER, B.A. Crown 8vo. 8s. 6d.

JONES.—*The Church of England and Common Sense.*
: By HARRY JONES, M.A. Fcap. 8vo. 3s. 6d.

JONES.—*Algebraical Exercises,*
: Progressively Arranged by the Rev. C. A. JONES, M.A. and C. H. CHEYNE, M.A. Mathematical Masters in Westminster School. 18mo. 2s. 6d.

Journal of Anatomy and Physiology.
: Conducted by Professors HUMPHRY and NEWTON, and Mr. CLARK of Cambridge; Professor TURNER, of Edinburgh; and Dr. WRIGHT, of Dublin. Published twice a year. Price to subscribers, 14s. per annum. Price 7s. 6d. each Part. Vol. 1, containing Parts I. and II. Royal 8vo. 16s. Part III. 6s.

JUVENAL, *for Schools.*
: With English Notes. By J. E. B. MAYOR, M.A. *New and Cheaper Edition.* Crown 8vo. [In the Press.

KEARY.—*The Little Wanderlin,*
> And other Fairy Tales. By A. and E. KEARY. 18mo. 3s. 6d.

KEMPIS (THOS. À).—*De Imitatione Christi. Libri IV.*
> Borders in the ancient style, after Holbein, Durer, and other old Masters, containing Dances of Death, Acts of Mercy, Emblems, and a variety of curious ornamentation. In white cloth, extra gilt. 7s. 6d.

KENNEDY.—*Legendary Fictions of the Irish Celts.*
> Collected and Narrated by PATRICK KENNEDY. Crown 8vo. 7s. 6d.

KINGSBURY.—*Spiritual Sacrifice and Holy Communion.*
> Seven Sermons preached during the Lent of 1867 at St. Leonard's-on-Sea, with Notes. By T. L. KINGSBURY, M.A. late Rector of Chetwynd. Fcap. 8vo. 3s. 6d.

KINGSLEY.— *Works by the Rev.* CHARLES KINGSLEY, M.A. *Rector of Eversley, and Canon of Chester.*

The Roman and the Teuton.
> A Series of Lectures delivered before the University of Cambridge. 8vo. 12s.

Two Years Ago.
> *Fourth Edition.* Crown 8vo. 6s.

"Westward Ho!"
> *Sixth Edition.* Crown 8vo. 6s.

Alton Locke.
> *New Edition.* With a New Preface. Crown 8vo. 4s. 6d.

Hypatia.
> *Fifth Edition.* Crown 8vo. 6s.

Yeast.
> *Fifth Edition.* Crown 8vo. 5s.

Hereward the Wake—Last of the English.
> Crown 8vo. 6s.

The Saint's Tragedy.
> *Third Edition.* Fcap. 8vo. 5s.

Andromeda,
> And other Poems. *Third Edition.* Fcap. 8vo. 5s.

The Water Babies.
> A Fairy Tale for a Land Baby. *New Edition*, with Illustrations by SIR NOEL PATON, R.S.A. and P. SKELTON. Crown 8vo. 6s.

The Heroes;
> Or, Greek Fairy Tales for my Children. With Coloured Illustrations. *New Edition.* 18mo. 4s. 6d.

KINGSLEY (Rev. CHARLES).—*Three Lectures delivered at the Royal Institution on the Ancien Régime.*
Crown 8vo. 6s.

The Water of Life,
And other Sermons. Fcap. 8vo. 6s.

Village Sermons.
Seventh Edition. Fcap. 8vo. 2s. 6d.

The Gospel of the Pentateuch.
Second Edition. Fcap. 8vo. 4s. 6d.

Good News of God.
Fourth Edition. Fcap. 8vo. 4s. 6d.

Sermons for the Times.
Third Edition. Fcap. 8vo. 3s. 6d.

Town and Country Sermons.
Extra fcap. 8vo. Second Edition. 6s.

Sermons on National Subjects.
First Series. Second Edition. Fcap. 8vo. 5s.
Second Series. Second Edition. Fcap. 8vo. 5s.

Discipline,
And other Sermons. Fcap. 8vo. 6s.

Alexandria and her Schools.
With a Preface. Crown 8vo. 5s.

The Limits of Exact Science as applied to History.
An Inaugural Lecture delivered before the University of Cambridge. Crown 8vo. 2s.

Phaethon; or, Loose Thoughts for Loose Thinkers.
Third Edition. Crown 8vo. 2s.

David.
Four Sermons: David's Weakness—David's Strength—David's Anger—David's Deserts. Fcap. 8vo. 2s. 6d.

KINGSLEY.— *Works by* HENRY KINGSLEY.
Austin Elliot.
New Edition. Crown 8vo. 6s.

The Recollections of Geoffry Hamlyn.
Second Edition. Crown 8vo. 6s.

The Hillyars and the Burtons:
A Story of Two Families. Crown 8vo. 6s.

Ravenshoe.
New Edition. Crown 8vo. 6s.

KINGSLEY (HENRY).—*Leighton Court.*
  New Edition. Crown 8vo. 6s.
  Silcote of Silcotes.
    Cheap Edition. [Shortly.
  Tales of Old Travel.
    Re-narrated. With Eight full-page Illustrations by HUARD. Crown 8vo. cloth extra gilt, 6s.

KIRCHHOFF.—*Researches on the Solar Spectrum and the Spectra of the Chemical Elements.*
  By G. KIRCHHOFF, of Heidelberg. Translated by HENRY E. ROSCOE, B.A. Second Part. 4to. 5s. with 2 Plates.

KITCHENER.—*Geometrical Note Book;*
  Containing Easy Problems in Geometrical Drawing, preparatory to the Study of Geometry. For the Use of Schools. By F. E. KITCHENER, M.A., Mathematical Master at Rugby. 4to. 2s.

LANCASTER.— *Works by* WILLIAM LANCASTER.
  Præterita.
    Poems. Extra fcap. 8vo. 4s. 6d.
  Studies in Verse.
    Extra fcap. 8vo. 4s. 6d.
  Eclogues and Mono-dramas; or, a Collection of Verses.
    Extra fcap. 8vo. 4s. 6d.

LATHAM.—*The Construction of Wrought-iron Bridges.*
  Embracing the Practical Application of the Principles of Mechanics to Wrought-Iron Girder Work. By J. H. LATHAM, Civil Engineer. 8vo. With numerous detail Plates. *Second Edition.* [Preparing.

LATHAM.—*Sertum Shaksperianum subnexis aliquot Aliunde excerptis Floribus.*
  Latinè reddidit H. LATHAM, A.M. Extra fcap. 8vo. 5s.

LATHAM.—*Black and White: A Three Months' Tour in the United States.*
  By H. LATHAM, M.A. Barrister-at-Law. 8vo. 10s. 6d.

LAW.—*The Alps of Hannibal.*
  By WILLIAM JOHN LAW, M.A. Two vols. 8vo. 21s.

Lectures to Ladies on Practical Subjects.
  Third Edition, revised. Crown 8vo. 7s. 6d.

LEMON.—*Legends of Number Nip.*
  By MARK LEMON. With Six Illustrations by CHARLES KEENE. Extra fcap. 8vo. 5s.

LIGHTFOOT. *Works by* J. B. LIGHTFOOT, D.D. *Hulsean Professor of Divinity in the University of Cambridge.*
St. Paul's Epistle to the Galatians.
A Revised Text, with Introduction, Notes, and Dissertations. Third Edition, revised. 8vo. 12s.
St. Paul's Epistle to the Philippians.
A Revised Text, with Introduction, Notes, and Dissertations Second Edition. 8vo. 12s.
St. Clement of Rome. The Two Epistles to the Corinthians
A Revised Text, with Introduction and Notes. 8vo. 8s. 6d.

Little Estella,
And other Fairy Tales for the Young. Royal 16mo. 3s. 6d.

LIVERPOOL.—*The Life and Administration of Robert Banks, Second Earl of Liverpool.*
Compiled from Original Documents by PROFESSOR YONGE. 3 vols. 8vo. 42s.

LOCKYER.—*Elementary Lessons in Astronomy. With numerous Illustrations.*
By J. NORMAN LOCKYER, F.R.S. 18mo. 5s. 6d.

LOWELL.—*Under the Willows, and other Poems.*
By JAMES RUSSELL LOWELL. Fcap. 8vo. 6s.

LUCKOCK.—*The Tables of Stone.*
A Course of Sermons preached in All Saints', Cambridge, by H. M. LUCKOCK, M.A., Vicar. Fcap. 8vo. 3s. 6d.

LUDLOW and HUGHES.—*A Sketch of the History of the United States from Independence to Secession.*
By J. M. LUDLOW, Author of "British India, its Races and its History," "The Policy of the Crown towards India," &c.
To which is added, "The Struggle for Kansas." By THOMAS HUGHES, Author of "Tom Brown's School Days," "Tom Brown at Oxford," &c. Crown 8vo. 8s. 6d.

LUSHINGTON.—*The Italian War, 1848-9, and the Last Italian Poet.*
By the late HENRY LUSHINGTON. With a Biographical Preface by G. S. VENABLES. Crown 8vo. 6s. 6d.

LYTTELTON.—*Works by* LORD LYTTELTON.
The Comus of Milton rendered into Greek Verse.
Extra fcap. 8vo. Second Edition. 5s.
The Samson Agonistes of Milton rendered into Greek Verse.
Extra fcap. 8vo. 6s. 6d.

MACCOLL.—*The Greek Sceptics from Pyrrho to Sextus.*
Being the Hare Prize Essay for 1868. By NORMAN MACCOLL, B.A. Downing College, Cambridge. Crown 8vo. 3s. 6d.

MACKENZIE.—*The Christian Clergy of the First Ten Centuries, and their Influence on European Civilization.*
By HENRY MACKENZIE, B.A. Scholar of Trinity College, Cambridge. Crown 8vo. 6s. 6d.

MACLAREN.—*Sermons preached at Manchester.*
By ALEXANDER MACLAREN. *Third Edition.* Fcap. 8vo. 4s. 6d.

A Second Series of Sermons.
Fcap. 8vo. 4s. 6d.

MACLAREN.—*Training, in Theory and Practice.*
By ARCHIBALD MACLAREN, Oxford. With Frontispiece, and other Illustrations. 8vo. Handsomely bound in cloth. 7s. 6d.

MACLEAR.—*Works by* G. F. MACLEAR, B.D. *Head Master of King's College School, and Preacher at the Temple Church :—*

A History of Christian Missions during the Middle Ages.
Crown 8vo. 10s. 6d.

The Witness of the Eucharist; or, The Institution and Early Celebration of the Lord's Supper, considered as an Evidence of the Historical Truth of the Gospel Narrative and of the Atonement.
Crown 8vo. 4s. 6d.

A Class-Book of Old Testament History.
With Four Maps. *Fourth Edition.* 18mo. 4s. 6d.

A Class-Book of New Testament History.
Including the connexion of the Old and New Testament. *Third Edition.* 18mo. 5s. 6d.

A Class-Book of the Catechism of the Church of England.
Second Edition. 18mo. cloth. 2s. 6d.

A Shilling Book of Old Testament History.
18mo. cloth limp. 1s.

A Shilling Book of New Testament History.
18mo. cloth limp. 1s.

MACLEAR (G. F.)—*A First Class-Book of the Catechism of the Church of England, with Scripture Proofs for Junior Classes and Schools.*
  18mo. 6d.

  The Order of Confirmation. A Sequel to the Class-Book of the Church Catechism, with Notes, and suitable Devotions.
  18mo. 3d.

MACMILLAN.—*Works by the Rev.* HUGH MACMILLAN.
  Bible Teachings in Nature.
    Third Edition. Crown 8vo. cloth, 6s.
  Foot-notes from the Page of Nature.
    With numerous Illustrations. Fcap. 8vo. 5s.
  Holidays on High Lands; or, Rambles and Incidents in Search of Alpine Plants.
    Crown 8vo. 6s.

Macmillan's Magazine.
  Published Monthly, price One Shilling. Volumes I.—XX. are now ready, 7s. 6d. each.

MACMILLAN & CO.'S *Six Shilling Series of Works of Fiction.*

KINGSLEY.—*Works by the* REV. CHARLES KINGSLEY, M.A.
  Westward Ho!
  Hypatia.
  Hereward the Wake—Last of the English.
  Two Years Ago.

Works by the Author of "The Heir of Redclyffe."
  The Heir of Redclyffe. Illustrated.
  Dynevor Terrace; or, The Clue of Life.
  Heartsease; or, The Brother's Wife. Illustrated.
  The Clever Woman of the Family.
  Hopes and Fears; or, Scenes from the Life of a Spinster.
  The Young Stepmother; or, A Chronicle of Mistakes.
  The Daisy Chain. Illustrated.
  The Trial: More Links of the Daisy Chain. Illustrated.

KINGSLEY.—*Works by* HENRY KINGSLEY.
   Geoffry Hamlyn.
   Ravenshoe.
   Austin Elliot.
   Hillyars and Burtons.
   Leighton Court.

TREVELYAN.—*Works by* G. O. TREVELYAN.
   Cawnpore.
   Competition Wallah.

MISCELLANEOUS.
   The Moor Cottage.
      By MAY BEVERLEY.
   Janet's Home.
   Tom Brown at Oxford.
      By the Author of "Tom Brown's School Days.
   Clemency Franklyn.
      By the Author of "Janet's Home."
   A Son of the Soil.
   Old Sir Douglas.
      By HON. MRS. NORTON.

MCCOSH.—*Works by* JAMES MCCOSH, LL.D. *President of Princeton College, New Jersey, U.S.*
   The Method of the Divine Government, Physical and Moral.
      Ninth Edition. 8vo. 10s. 6d.
   The Supernatural in Relation to the Natural.
      Crown 8vo. 7s. 6d.
   The Intuitions of the Mind.
      A New Edition. 8vo. 10s. 6d.
   An Examination of Mr. J. S. Mill's Philosophy.
      Being a Defence of Fundamental Truth. Crown 8vo. 7s. 6d.
   Philosophical Papers.
      1. Examination of Sir W. Hamilton's Logic. II. Reply to Mr. Mill's Third Edition. III. Present State of Moral Philosophy in Britain. 8vo. 3s. 6d.

MACPHERSON.—*The Baths and Wells of Europe.*
      Their Action and Uses, with Hints on Diet Cures, and Change of Air. By JOHN MACPHERSON, M.D. With Map. Extra fcap. 8vo. 6s. 6d.

LIST OF PUBLICATIONS.

Malbone; an Oldport Romance.
    By T. W. HIGGINSON. Fcap. 8vo. 2s. 6d.

MANSFIELD.—*Works by* C. B. MANSFIELD, M.A.
  Paraguay, Brazil, and the Plate.
    With a Map, and numerous Woodcuts. With a Sketch of his Life, by the Rev. CHARLES KINGSLEY. Crown 8vo. 12s. 6d.

  A Theory of Salts.
    A Treatise on the Constitution of Bipolar (two membered) Chemical Compounds. Crown 8vo. 14s.

MARKHAM.—*A History of the Abyssinian Expedition.*
    Including an Account of the Physical Geography, Geology, and Botany of the Region traversed by the English Forces. By CLEMENTS R. MARKHAM, F.S.A. With a Chapter by LIEUT. PRIDEAUX, containing a Narrative of the Mission and Captivity of Mr. Rassam and his Companions. With Maps, &c. 8vo. 14s.

MARRINER.—*Sermons preached at Lyme Regis.*
    By E. T. MARRINER, Curate. Fcap. 8vo. 4s. 6d.

MARSHALL.—*A Table of Irregular Greek Verbs.*
    8vo. 1s.

MARTIN.—*The Statesman's Year Book for* 1869. By FREDERICK MARTIN. (*Sixth Annual Publication.*)
    A Statistical, Mercantile, and Historical Account of the Civilized World for the Year 1868. Forming a Manual for Politicians and Merchants. *Third Edit.* Crown 8vo. 10s. 6d.

MARTINEAU.—*Biographical Sketches,* 1852–68.
    By HARRIET MARTINEAU. *Second Edition.* Crown 8vo. 8s. 6d.

MASSON.—*Works by* DAVID MASSON, M.A. *Professor of Rhetoric and English Literature in the University of Edinburgh.*

  Essays, Biographical and Critical.
    Chiefly on the English Poets. 8vo. 12s. 6d.

  British Novelists and their Styles.
    Being a Critical Sketch of the History of British Prose Fiction. Crown 8vo. 7s. 6d.

  Life of John Milton.
    Narrated in connexion with the Political, Ecclesiastical, and Literary History of his Time. Vol. I. with Portraits. 8vo. 18s.

  Recent British Philosophy.
    A Review, with Criticisms, including some Comments on Mr. Mill's Answer to Sir William Hamilton. *New and Cheaper Edition.* Crown 8vo. 6s.

MAUDSLEY.—*The Physiology and Pathology of the Mind.*
By HENRY MAUDSLEY, M.D. *New and Revised Edition.*
8vo. 16s.

MAURICE.—*Works by the Rev.* FREDERICK DENISON MAURICE, M.A. *Professor of Moral Philosophy in the University of Cambridge.*

The Conscience.
Lectures on Casuistry, delivered in the University of Cambridge. 8vo. 8s. 6d.

The Claims of the Bible and of Science.
A Correspondence on some Questions respecting the Pentateuch. Crown 8vo. 4s. 6d.

Dialogues on Family Worship.
Crown 8vo. 6s.

The Patriarchs and Lawgivers of the Old Testament.
Third and Cheaper Edition. Crown 8vo. 5s.
This volume contains Discourses on the Pentateuch, Joshua, Judges, and the beginning of the First Book of Samuel.

The Prophets and Kings of the Old Testament.
Second Edition. Crown 8vo. 10s. 6d.
This volume contains Discourses on Samuel I. and II.; Kings I. and II.; Amos, Joel, Hosea, Isaiah, Micah, Nahum, Habakkuk, Jeremiah, and Ezekiel.

The Gospel of the Kingdom of Heaven.
A Series of Lectures on the Gospel of St. Luke. Crown 8vo. 9s.

The Gospel of St. John.
A Series of Discourses. *Third and Cheaper Edition.* Crown 8vo. 6s.

The Epistles of St. John.
A Series of Lectures on Christian Ethics. *Second and Cheaper Edition.* Crown 8vo. 6s.

The Commandments considered as Instruments of National Reformation.
Crown 8vo. 4s. 6d.

Expository Sermons on the Prayer-book. The Prayer-book considered especially in reference to the Romish System.
Second Edition. Fcap. 8vo. 5s. 6d.

Lectures on the Apocalypse,
Or Book of the Revelation of St. John the Divine. Crown 8vo. 10s. 6d.

MAURICE.—*What is Revelation?*
    A Series of Sermons on the Epiphany; to which are added Letters to a Theological Student on the Bampton Lectures of Mr. MANSEL. Crown 8vo. 10s. 6d.

Sequel to the Inquiry, "What is Revelation?"
    Letters in Reply to Mr. Mansel's Examination of "Strictures on the Bampton Lectures." Crown 8vo. 6s.

Lectures on Ecclesiastical History.
    8vo. 10s. 6d.

Theological Essays.
    Second Edition. Crown 8vo. 10s. 6d.

The Doctrine of Sacrifice deduced from the Scriptures.
    Crown 8vo. 7s. 6d.

The Religions of the World,
    And their Relations to Christianity. Fourth Edition. Fcap. 8vo. 5s.

On the Lord's Prayer.
    Fourth Edition. Fcap. 8vo. 2s. 6d.

On the Sabbath Day;
    The Character of the Warrior; and on the Interpretation of History. Fcap. 8vo. 2s. 6d.

Learning and Working.
    Six Lectures on the Foundation of Colleges for Working Men. Crown 8vo. 5s.

The Ground and Object of Hope for Mankind.
    Four Sermons preached before the University of Cambridge. Crown 8vo. 3s. 6d.

Law's Remarks on the Fable of the Bees.
    With an Introduction by F. D. MAURICE, M.A. Fcap. 8vo. 4s. 6d.

MAYOR.—*A First Greek Reader.*
    Edited after Karl Halm, with Corrections and Additions. By the Rev. JOHN E. B. MAYOR, M.A. Fcap. 8vo. 6s.

Autobiography of Matthew Robinson.
    By JOHN E. B. MAYOR, M.A. Fcap. 8vo. 5s. 6d.

MAYOR.—*Greek for Beginners.*
    By the Rev. JOSEPH B. MAYOR, M.A. Fcap. 8vo. 4s. 6d.

Medicine in Modern Times.
    Discourses delivered at a Meeting of the British Medical Association at Oxford. By Dr. STOKES, Dr. ACLAND, Prof. ROLLESTON, Prof. HAUGHTON, and Dr. GULL. With a Report on Mercury by Dr. HUGHES BENNETT. Crown 8vo. 7s. 6d.

Merivale.—*Sallust for Schools.*
By C. Merivale, B.D. Second Edition. Fcap. 8vo. 4s. 6d.
*** The Jugurtha and the Catalina may be had separately, price 2s. 6d. each.

Keats' Hyperion rendered into Latin Verse.
By C. Merivale, B.D. Second Edition. Extra fcap. 8vo. 3s. 6d.

Milner.—*The Lily of Lumley.*
By Edith Milner. Crown 8vo. 7s. 6d.

Mistral, F.—*Mirelle, a Pastoral Epic of Provence.*
Translated by H. Crichton. Extra fcap. 8vo. 6s.

Modern Industries: A Series of Reports on Industry and Manufactures as represented in the Paris Exposition in 1867.
By Twelve British Workmen. Crown 8vo. 1s.

Moorhouse.—*Works by* James Moorhouse, M.A.
Some Modern Difficulties respecting the Facts of Nature and Revelation.
Fcap. 8vo. 2s. 6d.

The Hulsean Lectures for 1865.
Crown 8vo. 5s.

Morgan.—*A Collection of Mathematical Problems and Examples.*
By H. A. Morgan, M.A. Crown 8vo. 6s. 6d.

Morison.—*The Life and Times of Saint Bernard, Abbot of Clairvaux.*
By James Cotter Morison, M.A. New Edition, revised. Crown 8vo. 7s. 6d.

Morley, John.—*Edmund Burke—a Historical Study.*
Crown 8vo. 7s. 6d.

Morse.—*Working for God,*
And other Practical Sermons. By Francis Morse, M.A. Second Edition. Fcap. 8vo. 5s.

Morte D'Arthur.
Sir Thomas Malory's Book of King Arthur and of his noble Knights of the Round Table. The Edition of Caxton, revised for Modern use. With Introduction by Sir Edward Strachey Bart. Globe Series. Globe 8vo. 3s. 6d.

MULLINGER.—*Cambridge Characteristics in the Seventeenth Century.*
> By J. B. MULLINGER, B.A. Crown 8vo. 4s. 6d.

MURPHY.—*Habit and Intelligence, in their connexion with the Laws of Matter and Force.*
> A Series of Scientific Essays. By JOSEPH JOHN MURPHY. Two vols. 8vo. 16s.

MYERS.—*St. Paul.*
> A Poem. By F. W. H. MYERS. *Second Edition.* Extra fcap. 8vo. 2s. 6d.

MYERS.—*The Puritans.*
> A Poem. By ERNEST MYERS. Extra fcap. 8vo. 2s. 6d.

NETTLESHIP.—*Essays on Robert Browning's Poetry.*
> By JOHN T. NETTLESHIP. Extra fcap. 8vo. 6s. 6d.

New Landlord, The.
> Translated from the Hungarian of MAURICE JOKAI by A. J. PATTERSON. Two vols. crown 8vo. 21s.

NOEL.—*Beatrice, and other Poems.*
> By the Hon. RODEN NOEL. Fcap. 8vo. 6s.

Northern Circuit.
> Brief Notes of Travel in Sweden, Finland, and Russia. With Frontispiece. Crown 8vo. 5s.

NORTON.—*The Lady of La Garaye.*
> By the Hon. Mrs. NORTON. With Vignette and Frontispiece. *Sixth Edition.* Fcap. 8vo. 4s. 6d.

O'BRIEN.—*Works by* JAMES THOMAS O'BRIEN, D.D. *Bishop of Ossory.*

An Attempt to Explain and Establish the Doctrine of Justification by Faith only.
> *Third Edition.* 8vo. 12s.

Charge delivered at the Visitation in 1863.
> *Second Edition.* 8vo. 2s.

Old Sir Douglas.
> By the Hon. Mrs. NORTON. *Cheap Edition.* Crown 8vo. 6s

Oldbury.
> By MISS A. KEARY, Author of "Janet's Home." Three vols. crown 8vo. £1 11s. 6d.

OLIPHANT.—*Agnes Hopetoun's Schools and Holidays.*
> By Mrs. OLIPHANT. Royal 16mo. gilt leaves. 3s. 6d.

OLIVER.—*Lessons in Elementary Botany.*
> With nearly 200 Illustrations. By DANIEL OLIVER, F.R.S. F.L.S. 18mo. *Second Edition.* 4s. 6d.

OPPEN.—*French Reader,*
> For the Use of Colleges and Schools. By EDWARD A. OPPEN. Fcap. 8vo. 4s. 6d.

ORWELL.—*The Bishop's Walk and the Bishop's Times.*
> Poems on the Days of Archbishop Leighton and the Scottish Covenant. By ORWELL. Fcap. 8vo. 5s.

Our Year.
> A Child's Book, in Prose and Verse. By the Author of "John Halifax, Gentleman." Illustrated by CLARENCE DOBELL. Royal 16mo. 3s. 6d.

Oxford Spectator (The).
> Reprinted. Extra fcap. 8vo. 3s 6d.

PALGRAVE.—*History of Normandy and of England.*
> By Sir FRANCIS PALGRAVE. Completing the History to the Death of William Rufus. Vols. I. to IV. 8vo. each 21s.

PALGRAVE.—*A Narrative of a Year's Journey through Central and Eastern Arabia, 1862-3.*
> By WILLIAM GIFFORD PALGRAVE (late of the Eighth Regiment Bombay N.I.) *Fifth and Cheaper Edition.* With Map, Plans, and Portrait of Author, engraved on Steel by JEENS. Crown 8vo. 7s. 6d.

PALGRAVE.—Works by FRANCIS TURNER PALGRAVE, M.A. late Fellow of Exeter College, Oxford.

The Five Days' Entertainments at Wentworth Grange.
> A Book for Children. With Illustrations by ARTHUR HUGHES, and Engraved Title-page by JEENS. Small 4to. cloth extra. 9s.

The Golden Treasury of the best Songs and Lyrical Poems in the English Language.
> Selected and arranged, with Notes, by FRANCIS TURNER PALGRAVE. 18mo. cloth extra. 4s. 6d.

Essays on Art.
> Mulready—Dyce—Holman Hunt—Herbert—Poetry, Prose, and Sensationalism in Art—Sculpture in England—The Albert Cross, &c. Extra fcap. 8vo. 6s.

Sonnets and Songs.
> By WILLIAM SHAKESPEARE. Edited by F. T. PALGRAVE. GEM EDITION. With Vignette Title by JEENS. 3s. 6d.

Original Hymns.
> Second Edition, enlarged. 18mo. 1s. 6d.

PALGRAVE.—*The House of Commons.*
> Illustrations of its History and Practice. Lectures delivered at Reigate, Dec. 1868. By REGINALD F. D. PALGRAVE. With Notes and Index. Crown 8vo. 4s. 6d.

PALMER.—*The Book of Praise:*
> From the Best English Hymn Writers. Selected and arranged by SIR ROUNDELL PALMER. With Vignette by WOOLNER. 18mo. 4s. 6d. *Large Type Edition*, demy 8vo. 10s. 6d.

A Hymnal.
> Chiefly from the BOOK OF PRAISE. In various sizes.
> A.—In royal 32mo. cloth limp. 6d.
> B.—Small 18mo. larger type, cloth limp. 1s.
> C.—Same Edition, fine paper, cloth. 1s. 6d.
> An Edition with Music, Selected, Harmonized, and Composed by JOHN HULLAH. Square 18mo. 3s. 6d.

PARKES.—*Australian Views of England.*
> Eleven Letters written during the years 1861 and 1862. By HENRY PARKES, late Colonial Secretary of New South Wales. Crown 8vo. 3s. 6d.

PARKINSON.—*Works by* S. PARKINSON, B.D.

A Treatise on Elementary Mechanics.
> For the Use of the Junior Classes at the University and the Higher Classes in Schools. With a Collection of Examples. Fourth Edition, revised. Crown 8vo. 9s. 6d.

A Treatise on Optics.
> Second Edition, revised. Crown 8vo. 10s. 6d.

PATMORE.—*Works by* COVENTRY PATMORE.

The Angel in the House.
> Book I. The Betrothal.—Book II. The Espousals.—Book III. Faithful for Ever. With Tamerton Church Tower. Two vols. fcap. 8vo. 12s.
> *** A New and Cheap Edition, in one vol. fcap. 8vo. beautifully printed on toned paper, price 2s. 6d.

The Victories of Love.
> Fcap. 8vo. 4s. 6d.

PENROSE.—*On a Method of Predicting by Graphical Construction, Occultations of Stars by the Moon and Solar Eclipses for any given place.*
> Together with more Rigorous Methods for the accurate Calculation of Longitude. By F. C. PENROSE, F.R.A.S. With Charts, Tables, &c. 4to. 12s.

Phantasmagoria and other Poems.
> By LEWIS CARROLL, Author of "Alice's Adventures in Wonderland." Fcap. 8vo. gilt edges. 6s.

PHEAR.—*Elementary Hydrostatics.*
> By J. B. PHEAR, M.A. *Third Edition.* Crown 8vo. 5s. 6d.

PHILLIMORE.—*Private Law among the Romans.*
> From the Pandects. By JOHN GEORGE PHILLIMORE, Q.C. 8vo. 16s.

Philology.
　　The Journal of Sacred and Classical Philology. Four Vols. 8vo. 12s. 6d. each.
　　The Journal of Philology. New Series. Edited by W. G. CLARK, M.A. JOHN E. B. MAYOR, M.A. and W. ALDIS WRIGHT, M.A. Nos. I. II. and III. 8vo. 4s. 6d. each. (Half-yearly.)

PLATO.—*The Republic of Plato.*
　　Translated into English, with Notes. By Two Fellows of Trinity College, Cambridge (J. Ll. Davies, M.A. and D. J. Vaughan, M.A.). With Vignette Portraits of Plato and Socrates engraved by JEENS from an Antique Gem. (Golden Treasury Series.) *New Edition*, 18mo. 4s. 6d.

Platonic Dialogues, The,
　　For English Readers. By the late W. WHEWELL, D.D. F.R.S. Master of Trinity College, Cambridge. Vol. I. *Second Edition*, containing *The Socratic Dialogues*, fcap. 8vo. 7s. 6d.; Vol. II. containing *The Anti-Sophist Dialogues*, 6s. 6d.; Vol. III. containing *The Republic*, 7s. 6d.

PLAUTUS.—*The Mostellaria.*
　　With Notes, Prolegomena, and Excursus. By the late PROFESSOR RAMSAY. Edited by G. G. RAMSAY, M.A. 8vo. 14s.

Plea for a New English Version of the Scriptures.
　　By a Licentiate of the Church of Scotland. 8vo. 6s.

POPE.—*The Poetical Works of Alexander Pope.*
　　Edited, with Notes and Introductory Memoir, by PROFESSOR WARD. Globe Series. Globe 8vo. 3s. 6d.

POTTER.—*A Voice from the Church in Australia :*
　　Sermons preached in Melbourne. By the Rev. ROBERT POTTER, M.A. Extra fcap. 8vo. 4s. 6d.

POTTS.—*Hints towards Latin Prose Composition.*
　　By A. W. POTTS, M.A. Head Master of the Fettes School, Edinburgh. Extra fcap. 8vo. 2s. 6d.

Practitioner (The), a Monthly Journal of Therapeutics.
　　Edited by FRANCIS E. ANSTIE, M.D. 8vo. Price 1s. 6d. Vols. I. and II. 8vo. cloth. 10s. 6d. each.

PRATT.—*Treatise on Attractions, La Place's Functions, and the Figure of the Earth.*
　　By J. H. PRATT, M.A. *Third Edition.* Crown 8vo. 6s. 6d.

PRESCOTT.—*The Threefold Cord.*
　　Sermons preached before the University of Cambridge. By J. E. PRESCOTT, B.D. Fcap. 8vo. 3s. 6d.

PRESCOTT.—*Strong Drink and Tobacco Smoke; the Structure, Growth, and Uses of Malt, Hops, Yeast, and Tobacco.*
　　By HENRY P. PRESCOTT, F.L.S. With 167 Original Illustrations, engraved on Steel. 8vo. 7s. 6d.

LIST OF PUBLICATIONS. 37

PROCTER.—*A History of the Book of Common Prayer:*
With a Rationale of its Offices. *Eighth Edition, revised and enlarged.* Crown 8vo. 10s. 6d.

PROCTER AND MACLEAR.—*An Elementary Introduction to the Book of Common Prayer.*
Third Edition, Re-arranged, and Supplemented by an Explanation of the Morning and Evening Prayer and the Litany. By F. PROCTER, M.A. and G. F. MACLEAR, B.D. 18mo. 2s. 6d.

Psalms of David chronologically arranged.
An Amended Version, with Historical Introductions and Explanatory Notes. By FOUR FRIENDS. Crown 8vo. 10s. 6d.

PUCKLE.—*An Elementary Treatise on Conic Sections and Algebraic Geometry, with numerous Examples and Hints for their Solution,*
Especially designed for the Use of Beginners. By G. HALE PUCKLE, M.A. Head Master of Windermere College. *Third Edition, enlarged.* Crown 8vo. 7s. 6d.

PULLEN.—*The Psalter and Canticles, Pointed for Chanting,*
With Marks of Expression, and a List of Appropriate Chants. By the Rev. HENRY PULLEN, M.A. 8vo. 5s.

RALEGH.—*The Life of Sir Walter Ralegh, based upon Contemporary Documents.*
By EDWARD EDWARDS. Together with his LETTERS, now first Collected. With Portrait. Two Vols. 8vo. 32s.

RAMSAY.—*The Catechiser's Manual;*
Or, the Church Catechism Illustrated and Explained, for the Use of Clergymen, Schoolmasters, and Teachers. By ARTHUR RAMSAY, M.A. *Second Edition.* 18mo. 1s. 6d.

RAWLINSON.—*Elementary Statics.*
By G. RAWLINSON, M.A. Edited by EDWARD STURGES, M.A. Crown 8vo. 4s. 6d.

Rays of Sunlight for Dark Days.
A Book of Selections for the Suffering. With a Preface by C. J. VAUGHAN, D.D. 18mo. *New Edition.* 3s. 6d. Morocco, old style, 7s. 6d.

Reform.—*Essays on Reform.*
By the Hon. G. C. BRODRICK, R. H. HUTTON, LORD HOUGHTON, A. V. DICEY, LESLIE STEPHEN, J. B. KINNEAR, B. CRACROFT, C. H. PEARSON, GOLDWIN SMITH, JAMES BRYCE, A. L. RUTSON, and Sir GEO. YOUNG. 8vo. 10s. 6d.

Questions for a Reformed Parliament.
By F. H. HILL, GODFREY LUSHINGTON, MEREDITH TOWNSEND, W. L. NEWMAN, C. S. PARKER, J. B. KINNEAR, G. HOOPER, F. HARRISON, Rev. J. E. T. ROGERS, J. M. LUDLOW, and LLOYD JONES. 8vo. 10s. 6d.

REYNOLDS.—*A System of Medicine.* Vol. I.
    Edited by J. RUSSELL REYNOLDS, M.D. F.R.C.P. London. PART 1. GENERAL DISEASES, or Affections of the Whole System. § I.—Those determined by agents operating from without, such as the exanthemata, malarial diseases, and their allies. § II.—Those determined by conditions existing within the body, such as Gout, Rheumatism, Rickets, &c. PART II. LOCAL DISEASES, or Affections of particular Systems. § I.—Diseases of the Skin. 8vo. 25s.

A System of Medicine. Vol. II.
    PART II. § I.—Diseases of the Nervous System. A. General Nervous Diseases. B. Partial Diseases of the Nervous System. 1. Diseases of the Head. 2. Diseases of the Spinal Column. 3. Diseases of the Nerves. § II.—Diseases of the Digestive System. A. Diseases of the Stomach. 8vo. 25s.

A System of Medicine. Vol III.   [In the Press.

REYNOLDS.—*Notes of the Christian Life.*
    A Selection of Sermons by HENRY ROBERT REYNOLDS, B.A. President of Cheshunt College, and Fellow of University College, London. Crown 8vo. 7s. 6d.

REYNOLDS.—*Modern Methods in Elementary Geometry.*
    By E. M. REYNOLDS, M.A. Mathematical Master in Clifton College. Crown 8vo. 3s. 6d.

Ridicula Rediviva.
    Being old Nursery Rhymes. Illustrated in Colours by J. E. ROGERS. With Illuminated Cover. Imp. 4to. 9s.

ROBERTS.—*Discussions on the Gospels.*
    By the Rev. ALEXANDER ROBERTS, D.D. *Second Edition, revised and enlarged.* 8vo. 16s.

ROBERTSON.—*Pastoral Counsels.*
    By the late JOHN ROBERTSON, D.D. of Glasgow Cathedral. New Edition. With Preface by the Author of "Recreations of a Country Parson." Extra fcap. 8vo. 6s.

Robinson Crusoe.
    Edited after the Original Editions, with Introduction, by HENRY KINGSLEY. Globe Series. Globe 8vo. 3s. 6d.

ROBINSON.—*Diary, Reminiscences, and Correspondence of Henry Crabb Robinson, Barrister at Law, F.S.A.*
    Selected and Edited by Dr. T. SADLER. Three vols. 8vo. With Portrait. 36s.

ROBY.—*A Latin Grammar for the Higher Classes in Grammar Schools, based on the "Elementary Latin Grammar."*
    By H. J. ROBY, M.A.   [In the Press.

Roby.—*Story of a Household, and other Poems.*
> By Mary K. Roby. Fcap. 8vo. 5s.

Rogers.—*Historical Gleanings.*
> A Series of Sketches by J. E. Thorold Rogers. Contents: Montagu—Walpole—Adam Smith—Cobbett. Crown 8vo. 4s. 6d.

Romanis.—*Sermons preached at St. Mary's, Reading.*
> By William Romanis, M.A. First Series. Fcap. 8vo. Also, Second Series. 6s.

Roscoe.— *Works by* Professor Roscoe, F.R.S.

Lessons in Elementary Chemistry, Inorganic and Organic.
> Thirteenth Thousand. 18mo. 4s. 6d.

The Spectrum Analysis.
> A Series of Lectures delivered in 1868. With Four Appendices. Largely illustrated with Engravings, Maps, and Chromolithographs of the Spectra of the Chemical Elements and Heavenly Bodies. Medium 8vo. Cloth extra, gilt top, 21s.

Rossetti.— *Works by* Christina Rossetti.

Goblin Market, and other Poems.
> With Two Designs by D. G. Rossetti. *Second Edition.* Fcap. 8vo. 5s.

The Prince's Progress, and other Poems.
> With Two Designs by D. G. Rossetti. Fcap. 8vo. 6s.

Rossetti.— *Works by* William Michael Rossetti.

Dante's Comedy. The Hell.
> Translated into Literal Blank Verse. Fcap. 8vo. 5s.

Fine Art, chiefly Contemporary.
> Crown 8vo. 10s. 6d.

Routh.—*Treatise on Dynamics of Rigid Bodies*
> With Numerous Examples. By E. J. Routh, M.A. *New Edition.* Crown 8vo. 14s.

Rowsell.— *Works by* T. J. Rowsell, M.A.

The English Universities and the English Poor.
> Sermons preached before the University of Cambridge. Fcap. 8vo. 2s.

Man's Labour and God's Harvest.
> Sermons preached before the University of Cambridge in Lent, 1861. Fcap. 8vo. 3s.

Ruffini.—*Vincenzo; or, Sunken Rocks.*
> By John Ruffini. Three vols. crown 8vo. 31s. 6d.

Ruth and her Friends.
> A Story for Girls. With a Frontispiece. *Fourth Edition.* Royal 16mo. 3s. 6d.

SCOTT.—*The Poetical Works of Sir Walter Scott.*
>Edited, with Biographical and Critical Memoir, by FRANCIS TURNER PALGRAVE. Globe Series. Globe 8vo. 3s. 6d.

SCOTT.—*Discourses.*
>By A. J. SCOTT, M.A. late Professor of Logic in Owens College, Manchester. Crown 8vo. 7s. 6d.

Scouring of the White Horse.
>Or, the Long Vacation Ramble of a London Clerk. By the Author of "Tom Brown's School Days." Illustrated by DOYLE. *Eighth Thousand.* Imp. 16mo. 8s. 6d.

SEATON.—*A Hand-Book of Vaccination.*
>By EDWARD C. SEATON, M.D. Medical Inspector to the Privy Council. Extra fcap. 8vo. 8s. 6d.

SELKIRK.—*Guide to the Cricket Ground.*
>By G. H. SELKIRK. With Woodcuts. Extra Fcap. 8vo. 3s. 6d.

SELWYN.—*The Work of Christ in the World.*
>By G. A. SELWYN, D.D. Bishop of Lichfield. *Third Edition.* Crown 8vo. 2s.

SHAKESPEARE.—*The Works of William Shakespeare. Cambridge Edition.*
>Edited by WM. GEORGE CLARK, M.A. and W. ALDIS WRIGHT, M.A. Nine Vols. 8vo. cloth. 4l. 14s. 6d.

Shakespeare. Globe Edition.
>Edited by W. G. CLARK and W. A. WRIGHT. 91st *Thousand.* Globe 8vo. 3s. 6d.

Shakespeare's Tempest.
>With Glossarial and Explanatory Notes. By the Rev. J. M. JEPHSON. 18mo. 1s. 6d.

SHAIRP.—*Kilmahoe, and other Poems.*
>By J. CAMPBELL SHAIRP. Fcap. 8vo. 5s.

SHIRLEY.—*Elijah; Four University Sermons.*
>I. Samaria. II. Carmel. III. Kishon. IV. Horeb. By W.W. SHIRLEY, D.D. Fcap. 8vo. 2s. 6d.

SIMPSON.—*An Epitome of the History of the Christian Church.*
>By WILLIAM SIMPSON, M.A. *Fourth Edition.* Fcap. 8vo. 3s. 6d

SMITH.—*Works by* ALEXANDER SMITH.

A Life Drama, and other Poems.
>Fcap. 8vo. 2s. 6d.

City Poems.
>Fcap. 8vo. 5s.

Edwin of Deira.
>*Second Edition.* Fcap. 8vo. 5s.

SMITH.—*Poems by* CATHERINE BARNARD SMITH.
  Fcap. 8vo. 5s.

SMITH.—*Works by* GOLDWIN SMITH.
  A Letter to a Whig Member of the Southern Independence Association.
    Extra fcap. 8vo. 2s.
  Three English Statesmen; Pym, Cromwell, and Pitt.
    A Course of Lectures on the Political History of England. Extra fcap. 8vo. *New and Cheaper Edition.* 5s.

SMITH.—*Works by* BARNARD SMITH, M.A. *Rector of Glaston, Rutland, &c.*
  Arithmetic and Algebra.
    Tenth Edition. Crown 8vo. 10s. 6d.
  Arithmetic for the Use of Schools.
    Ninth Edition. Crown 8vo. 4s. 6d.
  A Key to the Arithmetic for Schools.
    Seventh Edition. Crown 8vo. 8s. 6d.
  Exercises in Arithmetic.
    With Answers. Cr. 8vo. limp cloth, 2s. 6d. Or sold separately as follows:—Part I. 1s. Part II. 1s. Answers, 6d.
  School Class Book of Arithmetic.
    18mo. 3s. Or sold separately, Parts I. and II. 10d. each. Part III. 1s.
  Keys to School Class Book of Arithmetic.
    Complete in One Volume, 18mo. 6s. 6d.; or Parts I. II. and III. 2s. 6d. each.
  Shilling Book of Arithmetic for National and Elementary Schools.
    18mo. cloth. Or separately, Part I. 2d.; II. 3d.; III. 7d.
  Answers to the Shilling Book of Arithmetic.
    18mo. 6d.
  Key to the Shilling Book of Arithmetic.
    18mo. 4s. 6d.
  Examination Papers in Arithmetic.
    In Four Parts. 18mo. 1s. 6d. With Answers, 1s. 9d.
  Key to Examination Papers in Arithmetic.
    18mo. 4s. 6d.

SMITH.—*Hymns of Christ and the Christian Life.*
  By the Rev. WALTER C. SMITH, M.A. Fcap. 8vo. 6s.

SMITH.—*Works by* W. S. SMITH, M.A. *Principal of St. Aidan's College, Birkenhead.*

Obstacles to Missionary Success among the Heathen.
The Maitland Prize Essay for 1867. Crown 8vo. 3s. 6d.

Christian Faith.
Sermons preached before the University of Cambridge. Fcap. 8vo. 3s. 6d.

SMITH.—*Works by* J. H. SMITH, M.A. *Gonville and Caius College, Cambridge.*

A Treatise on Elementary Statics.
Second Edition. Royal 8vo. 5s. 6d.

A Treatise on Elementary Trigonometry.
Royal 8vo. 5s.

A Treatise on Elementary Hydrostatics.
Royal 8vo. 4s. 6d.

A Treatise on Elementary Algebra.
For the use of Colleges and Schools. Crown 8vo. 6s. 6d.

SNOWBALL.—*The Elements of Plane and Spherical Trigonometry.*
By J. C. SNOWBALL, M.A. Tenth Edition. Crown 8vo. 7s. 6d.

Social Duties considered with Reference to the Organization of Effort in Works of Benevolence and Public Utility.
By a MAN OF BUSINESS. Fcap. 8vo. 4s. 6d.

SPENCER.—*Elements of Qualitative Chemical Analysis.*
By W. H. SPENCER, B.A. 4to. 10s. 6d.

Spenser's Complete Works.
Globe Edition. Edited by R. MORRIS, with Memoir by J. W. HALES. Globe 8vo. 3s. 6d.

Spring Songs.
By a WEST HIGHLANDER. With a Vignette Illustration by GOURLAY STEELE. Fcap. 8vo. 1s. 6d.

STEPHEN.—*General View of the Criminal Law of England.*
By J. FITZ-JAMES STEPHEN. 8vo. 18s.

STEWART AND LOCKYER.—*The Sun.*
By BALFOUR STEWART, F.R.S. and J. NORMAN LOCKYER, F.R.S. [Preparing.

STRATFORD DE REDCLIFFE.—*Shadows of the Past, in Verse.*
By VISCOUNT STRATFORD DE REDCLIFFE. Crown 8vo. 10s. 6d.

STRICKLAND.—*On Cottage Construction and Design.*
    By C. W. STRICKLAND. With Specifications and Plans. 8vo. 7s. 6d.

Sunday Library for Household Reading. Illustrated.
    Monthly Parts, 1s. ; Quarterly Vols. 4s. Gilt edges, 4s. 6d.
    Vol. I.—The Pupils of St. John the Divine, by the Author of "The Heir of Redclyffe."
    Vol. II.—The Hermits, by PROFESSOR KINGSLEY.
    Vol. III.—Seekers after God, by the Rev. F. W. FARRAR.
    Vol. IV.—England's Antiphon, by GEORGE MACDONALD, LL.D.
    Vol. V.—Great Christians of France, St. Louis and Calvin. By M. GUIZOT.
    Vol. VI.—Christian Singers of Germany, by CATHERINE WINKWORTH, Translator and Compiler of "Lyra Germanica."
    Vol. VII.—Apostles of Mediæval Europe, by the Rev. G. F. MACLEAR, B.D.
    Vol. VIII.—Alfred the Great, by THOMAS HUGHES, M.P.
                                                      [In December.

Sunday Library for 1868.
    4 Vols. Limp cloth, red Edges, in ornamental Box. Price 21s.

SWAINSON.—*Works by C. A. SWAINSON, D.D.*
    A Handbook to Butler's Analogy.
        Crown 8vo. 1s. 6d.
    The Creeds of the Church in their Relations to Holy Scripture and the Conscience of the Christian.
        8vo. cloth. 9s.
    The Authority of the New Testament,
        And other Lectures, delivered before the University of Cambridge. 8vo. cloth. 12s.

TACITUS.—*The History of Tacitus translated into English.*
    By A. J. CHURCH, M.A. and W. J. BRODRIBB, M.A. With a Map and Notes. 8vo. 10s. 6d.
    The Agricola and Germany.
        By the same Translators. With Map and Notes. Fcap. 8vo. 2s. 6d.
    The Agricola and Germania.
        A Revised Text. With English Notes and Maps. By A. J. CHURCH, M.A. and W. J. BRODRIBB. Fcap. 8vo. 3s. 6d.
        The *Agricola* and *Germania* may be had separately, price 2s. each.

TAIT AND STEELE.—*A Treatise on Dynamics.*
    With numerous Examples. By P. G. TAIT and W. J. STEELE. Second Edition. Crown 8vo. 10s. 6d.

TAYLOR.—*Words and Places;*
Or, Etymological Illustrations of History, Ethnology, and Geography. By the Rev. ISAAC TAYLOR. *Second Edition.* Crown 8vo. 12s. 6d.

TAYLOR.—*The Restoration of Belief.*
New and Revised Edition. By ISAAC TAYLOR, Esq. Crown 8vo. 8s. 6d.

TAYLOR (C.).—*Geometrical Conics.*
By C. TAYLOR, B.A. Crown 8vo. 7s. 6d.

TEBAY.—*Elementary Mensuration for Schools,*
With numerous Examples. By SEPTIMUS TEBAY, B.A. Head Master of Queen Elizabeth's Grammar School, Rivington. Extra fcap. 8vo. 3s. 6d.

TEMPLE.—*Sermons preached in the Chapel of Rugby School.*
By F. TEMPLE, D.D. Head Master. *New and Cheaper Edition.* Crown 8vo. 7s. 6d.

THORNTON.—*On Labour; its Wrongful Claims and Rightful Dues, Actual Present and Possible Future.*
By W. T. THORNTON, Author of "A Plea for Peasant Proprietors." 8vo. 14s.

THORPE.—*Diplomatarium Anglicum Ævi Saxonici.*
A Collection of English Charters, from the Reign of King Æthelberht of Kent, A.D. DCV. to that of William the Conqueror. With a Translation of the Anglo-Saxon. By BENJAMIN THORPE, Member of the Royal Academy of Sciences, Munich. 8vo. cloth. 21s.

THRING.—*Works by* EDWARD THRING, *M.A. Head Master of Uppingham.*

A Construing Book.
Fcap. 8vo. 2s. 6d.

A Latin Gradual.
A First Latin Construing Book for Beginners. 18mo. 2s. 6d.

The Elements of Grammar taught in English.
Fourth Edition. 18mo. 2s.

The Child's Grammar.
A New Edition. 18mo. 1s.

Sermons delivered at Uppingham School.
Crown 8vo. 5s.

School Songs.
With the Music arranged for Four Voices. Edited by the Rev. EDWARD THRING, M.A. and H. RICCIUS. Small folio. 7s. 6d.

THRING.—*Education and School.*
   Second Edition. Crown 8vo. 6s.
A Manual of Mood Constructions.
   Extra fcap. 8vo. 1s. 6d.

THRUPP.—*Works by the Rev. J. F. THRUPP.*
The Song of Songs.
   A New Translation, with a Commentary and an Introduction. Crown 8vo. 7s. 6d.
Introduction to the Study and Use of the Psalms.
   Two Vols. 8vo. 21s.
Psalms and Hymns for Public Worship.
   Selected and Edited by the Rev. J. F. THRUPP, M.A. 18mo. 2s. Common paper, 1s. 4d.
The Burden of Human Sin as borne by Christ.
   Three Sermons preached before the University of Cambridge in Lent, 1865. Crown 8vo. 3s. 6d.

THUCYDIDES.—*The Sicilian Expedition:*
   Being Books VI. and VII. of Thucydides, with Notes. By the Rev. PERCIVAL FROST, M.A. Fcap. 8vo. 5s.

TOCQUEVILLE.—*Memoir, Letters, and Remains of Alexis de Tocqueville.*
   Translated from the French by the Translator of "Napoleon's Correspondence with King Joseph." With numerous Additions. Two vols. Crown 8vo. 21s.

TODD.—*The Books of the Vaudois.*
   The Waldensian Manuscripts preserved in the Library of Trinity College, Dublin, with an Appendix by JAMES HENTHORN TODD, D.D. Crown 8vo. cloth. 6s.

TODHUNTER.—*Works by* ISAAC TODHUNTER, M.A. F.R.S.
Euclid for Colleges and Schools.
   New Edition. 18mo. 3s. 6d.
Algebra for Beginners.
   With numerous Examples. New Edition. 18mo. 2s. 6d.
Key to Algebra for Beginners.
   Crown 8vo. 6s. 6d.
Mechanics for Beginners.
   With numerous Examples. 18mo. 4s. 6d.
Trigonometry for Beginners.
   With numerous Examples. Second Edition. 18mo. 2s. 6d.

TODHUNTER.—*Mensuration for Beginners.*
  With numerous examples. 18mo. 2s. 6d.

  A Treatise on the Differential Calculus.
    With numerous Examples. *Fourth Edition.* Crown 8vo. 10s. 6d.

  A Treatise on the Integral Calculus.
    With numerous Examples. *Third Edition.* Crown 8vo. 10s. 6d.

  A Treatise on Analytical Statics.
    Third Edition. Crown 8vo. 10s. 6d.

  A Treatise on Conic Sections.
    Fourth Edition. Crown 8vo. 7s. 6d.

  Algebra for the Use of Colleges and Schools.
    Fourth Edition. Crown 8vo. 7s. 6d.

  Plane Trigonometry for Colleges and Schools.
    Third Edition. Crown 8vo. 5s.

  A Treatise on Spherical Trigonometry for the Use of Colleges and Schools.
    Second Edition. Crown 8vo. 4s. 6d.

  Critical History of the Progress of the Calculus of Variations during the Nineteenth Century.
    8vo. 12s.

  Examples of Analytical Geometry of Three Dimensions.
    Second Edition. Crown 8vo. 4s.

  A Treatise on the Theory of Equations.
    Second Edition. Crown 8vo. 7s. 6d.

  Mathematical Theory of Probability.
    8vo. 18s.

Tom Brown's School Days.
  By an OLD BOY. Fcap. 8vo. 5s.
  Golden Treasury Edition, 4s. 6d.
  PEOPLE'S EDITION, 2s.
  Illustrated Edition. By A. HUGHES and SYDNEY HALL. Square. 12s.

Tom Brown at Oxford.
  By the Author of "Tom Brown's School Days." *New Edition.* Crown 8vo. 6s.

Tracts for Priests and People. (*By various Writers.*)
  THE FIRST SERIES, Crown 8vo. 8s.
  THE SECOND SERIES, Crown 8vo. 8s.
  The whole Series of Fifteen Tracts may be had separately, price One Shilling each.

TRENCH.—*Works by* R. CHENEVIX TRENCH, D.D. *Archbishop of Dublin.*

Notes on the Parables of Our Lord.
  Tenth Edition. 8vo. 12s.

Notes on the Miracles of Our Lord.
  Eighth Edition. 8vo. 12s.

Synonyms of the New Testament.
  New Edition. One vol. 8vo. cloth. 10s. 6d.

On the Study of Words.
  Thirteenth Edition. Enlarged and Revised. Fcap. 8vo. 4s. 6d.

English Past and Present.
  Sixth Edition. Enlarged and Revised. Fcap. 8vo. 4s. 6d.

Proverbs and their Lessons.
  Sixth Edition. Enlarged. Fcap. 8vo. 3s. 6d.

Select Glossary of English Words used formerly in Senses different from the present.
  Third Edition. Fcap. 8vo. 4s.

On some Deficiencies in our English Dictionaries.
  Second Edition. 8vo. 3s.

Sermons preached in Westminster Abbey.
  Second Edition. 8vo. 10s. 6d.

The Fitness of Holy Scripture for Unfolding the Spiritual Life of Man:
  Christ the Desire of all Nations; or, the Unconscious Prophecies of Heathendom. Hulsean Lectures. Fcap. 8vo. *Fourth Edition.* 5s.

On the Authorized Version of the New Testament.
  Second Edition. 8vo. 7s.

Justin Martyr, and other Poems.
  Fifth Edition. Fcap. 8vo. 6s.

Gustavus Adolphus.—Social Aspects of the Thirty Years' War.
  Fcap. 8vo. 2s. 6d.

Poems.
  Collected and arranged anew. Fcap. 8vo. 7s. 6d.

Poems from Eastern Sources, Genoveva and other Poems.
  Second Edition. Fcap. 8vo. 5s. 6d.

Elegiac Poems.
  Third Edition. Fcap. 8vo. 2s. 6d.

TRENCH (R. CHENEVIX)—*Calderon's Life's a Dream :*
 The Great Theatre of the World. With an Essay on his Life and Genius. Fcap. 8vo. 4s. 6d.

Remains of the late Mrs. Richard Trench.
 Being Selections from her Journals, Letters, and other Papers. *New and Cheaper Issue.* With Portrait. 8vo. 6s.

Commentary on the Epistles to the Seven Churches in Asia.
 Third Edition, revised. 8vo. 8s. 6d.

Sacred Latin Poetry.
 Chiefly Lyrical. Selected and arranged for Use. *Second Edition* Corrected and Improved. Fcap. 8vo. 7s.

Studies in the Gospels.
 Second Edition. 8vo. 10s. 6d.

The Sermon on the Mount.
 An Exposition drawn from the writings of St. Augustine, with an Essay on his merits as an Interpreter of Holy Scripture. *Third Edition.* Enlarged. 8vo. 10s. 6d.

Shipwrecks of Faith :
 Three Sermons preached before the University of Cambridge in May, 1867. Fcap. 8vo. 2s. 6d.

A Household Book of English Poetry.
 Selected and Arranged with Notes. By the ARCHBISHOP OF DUBLIN. Extra fcap. 8vo. 5s. 6d.

TRENCH (Rev. FRANCIS).—*Brief Notes on the Greek of the New Testament (for English Readers).*
 Crown 8vo. cloth. 6s.

TRENCH (CAPTAIN F.).—*The Russo-Indian Question Historically, Strategically, and Politically Considered.*
 With a Sketch of Central Asiatic Politics. By Captain F. TRENCH, F.R.G.S. 20th Hussars. With Map. Crown 8vo. 7s. 6d.

TREVELYAN.—*Works by* G. O. TREVELYAN, M.P.

The Competition Wallah.
 New Edition. Crown 8vo. 6s.

Cawnpore,
 Illustrated with Plan. *Second Edition.* Crown 8vo. 6s.

TUDOR.—*The Decalogue viewed as the Christian's Law.*
 With Special Reference to the Questions and Wants of the Times. By the Rev. RICH. TUDOR, B.A. Crown 8vo. 10s. 6d.

LIST OF PUBLICATIONS.

TULLOCH.—*The Christ of the Gospels and the Christ of Modern Criticism.*
Lectures on M. RENAN'S "Vie de Jésus." By JOHN TULLOCH, D.D. Principal of the College of St. Mary, in the University of St. Andrew. Extra fcap. 8vo. 4s. 6d.

TURNER.—*Sonnets.*
By the Rev. CHARLES TENNYSON TURNER. Dedicated to his Brother, the Poet Laureate. Fcap. 8vo. 4s. 6d.

Small Tableaux.
By the Rev. C. TURNER. Fcap. 8vo. 4s. 6d.

Twelve Parables of Our Lord.
Illustrated in Colours from Sketches taken in the East by McENIRY, with Frontispiece from a Picture by JOHN JELLICOE, and Illuminated Texts and Borders. Royal 4to. in Ornamental Binding. 42s.

TYRWHITT.—*The Schooling of Life.*
By R. ST. JOHN TYRWHITT. M.A. Vicar of St. Mary Magdalen, Oxford. Fcap. 8vo. 3s. 6d.

Vacation Tourists;
And Notes of Travel in 1861. Edited by F. GALTON, F.R.S. With Ten Maps illustrating the Routes. 8vo. 14s.

Vacation Tourists;
And Notes of Travel in 1862 and 1863. Edited by FRANCIS GALTON, F.R.S. 8vo. 16s.

VANDERVELL AND WITHAM.—*A System of Figure Skating.*
Being the Theory and Practice of the Art as developed in England, with a Glance at its Origin and History. By H. E. VANDERVELL and T. M. WITHAM, Members of the London Skating Club. Extra fcap. 8vo. 6s.

VAUGHAN.—*Works by* CHARLES J. VAUGHAN, D.D. *Master of the Temple.*

Notes for Lectures on Confirmation.
With suitable Prayers. *Seventh Edition.* Fcap. 8vo. 1s. 6d.

Lectures on the Epistle to the Philippians.
Second Edition. Crown 8vo. 7s. 6d.

Lectures on the Revelation of St. John.
Third Edition. Two vols. [In the Press.

Epiphany, Lent, and Easter.
A Selection of Expository Sermons. *Third Edition.* Crown 8vo. 10s. 6d.

VAUGHAN (CHARLES J.).—*The Book and the Life*,
And other Sermons, preached before the University of Cambridge. *New Edition.* Fcap. 8vo. 4s. 6d.

Memorials of Harrow Sundays.
A Selection of Sermons preached in Harrow School Chapel. With a View of the Chapel. *Fourth Edition.* Crown 8vo. 10s. 6d.

St. Paul's Epistle to the Romans.
The Greek Text with English Notes. *New Edition in the Press.*

Twelve Discourses on Subjects connected with the Liturgy and Worship of the Church of England.
Fcap. 8vo. 6s.

Lessons of Life and Godliness.
A Selection of Sermons preached in the Parish Church of Doncaster. *Third Edition.* Fcap. 8vo. 4s. 6d.

Words from the Gospels.
A Second Selection of Sermons preached in the Parish Church of Doncaster. *Second Edition.* Fcap. 8vo. 4s. 6d.

The Epistles of St. Paul.
For English Readers. Part I. containing the First Epistle to the Thessalonians. *Second Edition.* 8vo. 1s. 6d. Each Epistle will be published separately.

Lessons of the Cross and Passion.
Six Lectures delivered in Hereford Cathedral during the Week before Easter 1869. Fcap. 8vo. 2s. 6d.

The Church of the First Days.
Series I. The Church of Jerusalem. *Second Edition.*
„ II. The Church of the Gentiles. *Second Edition.*
„ III. The Church of the World. *Second Edition.*
Fcap. 8vo. cloth. 4s. 6d. each.

Life's Work and God's Discipline.
Three Sermons. Fcap. 8vo. cloth. 2s. 6d.

The Wholesome Words of Jesus Christ.
Four Sermons preached before the University of Cambridge in November, 1866. Fcap. 8vo. cloth. 3s. 6d. *Second Edition.*

Foes of Faith.
Sermons preached before the University of Cambridge in November, 1868. Fcap. 8vo. 3s. 6d.

VAUGHAN.—*Works by* DAVID J. VAUGHAN, M.A. *Vicar of St. Martin's, Leicester.*

Sermons preached in St. John's Church, Leicester,
During the Years 1855 and 1856. Crown 8vo. 5s. 6d.

Sermons on the Resurrection.
With a Preface. Fcap. 8vo. 3s.

Three Sermons on the Atonement.
1s. 6d.

Sermons on Sacrifice and Propitiation.
2s. 6d.

Christian Evidences and the Bible.
New Edition. Revised and enlarged. Fcap. 8vo. cloth. 5s. 6d.

VAUGHAN.—*Memoir of Robert A. Vaughan,*
Author of "Hours with the Mystics." By ROBERT VAUGHAN, D.D. Second Edition. Revised and enlarged. Extra fcap. 8vo. 5s.

VENN.—*The Logic of Chance.*
An Essay on the Foundations and Province of the Theory of Probability, with special reference to its application to Moral and Social Science. By the Rev. J. VENN, M.A. Fcap. 8vo. 7s. 6d.

Village Sermons.
By a NORTHAMPTONSHIRE RECTOR. With a Preface on the Inspiration of Holy Scripture. Crown 8vo. 6s.

Vittoria Colonna.—Life and Poems.
By MRS. HENRY ROSCOE. Crown 8vo. 9s.

Volunteer's Scrap Book.
By the Author of "The Cambridge Scrap Book." Crown 4to. 7s. 6d.

WAGNER.—*Memoir of the Rev. George Wagner,*
late of St. Stephen's, Brighton. By J. N. SIMPKINSON, M.A. Third and Cheaper Edition. 5s.

WALLACE.—*The Malay Archipelago: The Land of the Orang Utan and the Bird of Paradise.*
A Narrative of Travel. With Studies of Man and Nature. By ALFRED RUSSEL WALLACE. With Maps and Illustrations. Second Edition. Two Vols. crown 8vo. 24s.

WARD.—*The House of Austria in the Thirty Years' War.*
Two Lectures. With Illustrative Notes. By A. W. WARD, M.A. Professor of History in Owens College, Manchester. Extra Fcap. 8vo. 2s. 6d.

WARREN.—*An Essay on Greek Federal Coinage.*
    By the Hon. J. LEICESTER WARREN, M.A. 8vo. 2s. 6d.

WEBSTER.—*Works by* AUGUSTA WEBSTER.
  Dramatic Studies.
    Extra fcap. 8vo. 5s.
  A Woman Sold,
    And other Poems. Crown 8vo. 7s. 6d.
  Prometheus Bound, of Æschylus,
    Literally Translated into English Verse. Extra fcap. 8vo. 3s. 6d.
  Medea of Euripides,
    Literally Translated into English Verse. Extra fcap. 8vo. 3s. 6d.

WESTCOTT.—*Works by* BROOKE FOSS WESTCOTT. B.D.
    Canon of Peterborough.
  A General Survey of the History of the Canon of the New Testament during the First Four Centuries.
    Third Edition, revised.   [In the Press.
  Characteristics of the Gospel Miracles.
    Sermons preached before the University of Cambridge. *With Notes.* Crown 8vo. 4s. 6d.
  Introduction to the Study of the Four Gospels.
    Third Edition. Crown 8vo. 10s. 6d.
  The Gospel of the Resurrection.
    Thoughts on its Relation to Reason and History. *New Edition.* Fcap. 8vo. 4s. 6d.
  The Bible in the Church.
    A Popular Account of the Collection and Reception of the Holy Scriptures in the Christian Churches. *Second Edition.* 18mo. 4s. 6d.
  A General View of the History of the English Bible.
    Crown 8vo. 10s. 6d.
  The Christian Life, Manifold and One.
    Six Sermons preached in Peterborough Cathedral. Crown 8vo. 2s. 6d.

Westminster Plays.
    Lusus Alteri Westmonasterienses, Sive Prologi et Epilogi ad Fabulas in Sti Petri Collegio: actas qui Exstabant collecti et justa quoad licuit annorum serie ordinati, quibus accedit Declamationum quæ vocantur et Epigrammatum Delectus. Curantibus J. MURE, A.M., H. BULL, A.M., C. B. SCOTT, B.D. 8vo. 12s. 6d.
    IDEM.—Pars Secunda, 1820—1865. Quibus accedit Epigrammatum Delectus. 8vo. 15s.

LIST OF PUBLICATIONS.

WILKINS.—*The Light of the World.*
An Essay by A. S. WILKINS, M.A. Professor of Latin in Owens College, Manchester. Crown 8vo. 3s. 6d.

WILSON.—*Works by* GEORGE WILSON, M.D.

Counsels of an Invalid.
Letters on Religious Subjects. With Vignette Portrait. Fcap. 8vo. 4s. 6d.

Religio Chemici.
With a Vignette beautifully engraved after a Design by Sir NOEL PATON. Crown 8vo. 8s. 6d.

WILSON (GEORGE).—*The Five Gateways of Knowledge.*
New Edition. Fcap. 8vo. 2s. 6d. Or in Paper Covers, 1s.

The Progress of the Telegraph.
Fcap. 8vo. 1s.

WILSON.—*An English, Hebrew, and Chaldee Lexicon and Concordance.*
By WILLIAM WILSON, D.D. Canon of Winchester. *Second Edition.* 4to. 25s.

WILSON.—*Memoir of George Wilson,* M.D. F.R.S.E.
Regius Professor of Technology in the University of Edinburgh. By HIS SISTER. *New Edition.* Crown 8vo. 6s.

WILSON.—*A Treatise on Dynamics.*
By W. P. WILSON, M.A. 8vo. 9s. 6d.

WILSON.—*Works by* DANIEL WILSON, LL.D.

Prehistoric Annals of Scotland.
New Edition. With numerous Illustrations. Two Vols. demy 8vo. 36s.

Prehistoric Man.
New Edition. Revised and partly re-written, with numerous Illustrations. One vol. 8vo. 21s.

WILSON.—*Elementary Geometry.*
Angles, Parallels, Triangles, Equivalent Figures, the Circle, and Proportion. By J. M. WILSON, M.A. Fellow of St. John's College, Cambridge, and Mathematical Master at Rugby. *Second Edition.* Extra fcap. 8vo. 3s. 6d.
PART II.—The Circle and Proportion. Extra fcap. 8vo. 2s. 6d.

WINSLOW.—*Force and Nature. Attraction and Repulsion.*
The Radical Principles of Energy graphically discussed in their Relations to Physical and Morphological Development. By C. F. WINSLOW, M.D. 8vo. 14s.

WOLLASTON.—*Lyra Devoniensis.*
> By T. V. WOLLASTON, M.A. Fcap. 8vo. 3s. 6d.

WOLSELEY.—*The Soldier's Pocket Book for Field Service.*
> By Colonel G. J. WOLSELEY, Deputy Quartermaster-General in Canada. 16mo. roan. 5s.

WOLSTENHOLME.—*A Book of Mathematical Problems.*
> Crown 8vo. 8s. 6d.

Woman's Culture and Woman's Work.
> A Series of Essays, by FRANCES POWER COBBE, C. PEARSON, JESSIE BOUCHERETT, SOPHIA JEX-BLAKE, Rev. G. BUTLER, ELIZABETH WOLSTENHOLME, JAMES STUART, M.A. *Fellow of Trinity College, Cambridge,* HERBERT MOZLEY, *Barrister-at-Law,* J. BOYD-KINNEAR, *Barrister-at-Law,* and JULIA WEDGWOOD. Edited by JOSEPHINE E. BUTLER. 8vo. 10s. 6d.

WOODFORD.—*Christian Sanctity.*
> By JAMES RUSSELL WOODFORD, M.A. Fcap. 8vo. cloth. 3s.

WOODWARD.— *Works by the Rev.* HENRY WOODWARD, *edited by his Son,* THOMAS WOODWARD, M.A. *Dean of Down.*

> *Essays, Thoughts and Reflections, and Letters.*
>> Fifth Edition. Crown 8vo. 10s. 6d.

> *The Shunammite.*
>> Second Edition. Crown 8vo. 10s. 6d.

> *Sermons.*
>> Fifth Edition. Crown 8vo. 10s. 6d.

WOOLLEY.—*Lectures delivered in Australia.*
> By the late JOHN WOOLLEY, D.C.L. Crown 8vo. 8s. 6d.

WOOLNER.—*My Beautiful Lady.*
> By THOMAS WOOLNER. With a Vignette by ARTHUR HUGHES. Third Edition. Fcap. 8vo. 5s.

Words from the Poets.
> Selected by the Editor of "Rays of Sunlight." With a Vignette and Frontispiece. 18mo. Extra cloth gilt. 2s. 6d. *Cheaper Edition,* 18mo. limp. 1s.

Worship (The) of God and Fellowship among Men.
> Sermons on Public Worship. By PROFESSOR MAURICE, and Others. Fcap. 8vo. 3s. 6d.

WORSLEY.—*Christian Drift of Cambridge Work.*
> Eight Lectures. By T. WORSLEY, D.D. Master of Downing College, Cambridge. Crown 8vo. cloth. 6s.

WRIGHT.—*Works by* J. WRIGHT, M.A.

Hellenica;
Or, a History of Greece in Greek, as related by Diodorus and Thucydides, being a First Greek Reading Book, with Explanatory Notes Critical and Historical. *Third Edition.* WITH A VOCABULARY. 12mo. 3s. 6d.

The Seven Kings of Rome.
An Easy Narrative, abridged from the First Book of Livy by the omission of difficult passages, being a First Latin Reading Book, with Grammatical Notes. Fcap. 8vo. 3s.

A Vocabulary and Exercises on the " Seven Kings of Rome."
Fcap. 8vo. 2s. 6d.
*** The Vocabulary and Exercises may also be had bound up with "The Seven Kings of Rome." Price 5s.

A Help to Latin Grammar;
Or, the Form and Use of Words in Latin, with Progressive Exercises. Crown 8vo. 4s. 6d.

David, King of Israel.
Readings for the Young. With Six Illustrations. Royal 16mo. cloth, gilt. 3s. 6d.

WURTZ.—*A History of Chemical Theory from the Age of Lavoisier down to the present Time.*
Translated by HENRY WATTS, F.R.S. Crown 8vo. 6s.

YOUMANS.—*Modern Culture,*
Its True Aims and Requirements. A Series of Addresses and Arguments on the Claims of Scientific Education. Edited by EDWARD L. YOUMANS, M.D. Crown 8vo. 8s. 6d.

Works by the Author of
"THE HEIR OF REDCLYFFE."

The Chaplet of Pearls. Two Vols. Crown 8vo. 12s.

The Prince and the Page. A Book for the Young. 18mo. 3s. 6d.

A Book of Golden Deeds. 18mo. 4s. 6d. Cheap Edition, 1s.

History of Christian Names. Two Vols. Crown 8vo. 1l. 1s.

The Heir of Redclyffe. Seventeenth Edition. With Illustrations. Crown 8vo. 6s.

Dynevor Terrace. Third Edition. Crown 8vo. 6s.

The Daisy Chain. Ninth Edition. With Illustrations. Crown 8vo. 6s.

The Trial: More Links of the Daisy Chain. Fourth Edition. With Illustrations. Crown 8vo. 6s.

Heartsease. Tenth Edition. With Illustrations. Crown 8vo. 6s.

Hopes and Fears. Third Edition. Crown 8vo. 6s.

The Young Stepmother. Third Edition. Crown 8vo. 6s.

The Lances of Lynwood. With Coloured Illustrations. Second Edition. Extra fcap. cloth. 4s. 6d.

The Little Duke. New Edition. 18mo. cloth. 3s. 6d.

Clever Woman of the Family. Crown 8vo. 6s.

Danvers Papers; an Invention. Crown 8vo. 4s. 6d.

Dove in the Eagle's Nest. Two vols. Crown 8vo. 12s.

Cameos from English History. From Rollo to Edward II. Extra fcap. 8vo. 5s.

A Book of Worthies; gathered from the Old Histories and Written Anew. 18mo. cloth extra. 4s. 6d.

www.ingramcontent.com/pod-product-compliance
Lightning Source LLC
Chambersburg PA
CBHW031451160426
43195CB00010BB/935